Young Vic

Public Enemy

by Henrik Ibsen

in a new version by David Harrower

This production opened at the Young Vic on 4 May 2013.

Public Enemy

by Henrik Ibsen

in a new version by David Harrower

Aslaksen	**Niall Ashdown**
Horster	**Adam Best**
Hovstad	**Bryan Dick**
Mayor	**Darrell D'Silva**
Stockmann	**Nick Fletcher**
Billing	**Joel Fry**
Mrs Stockmann	**Charlotte Randle**
Morten Kiil	**David Sibley**
Petra	**Beatrice Walker**
Eilif	**Reece Donn**
	Domenico Frescofiore
Morten	**Sasha Gray**
	Kai Hill

Direction	**Richard Jones**
Design	**Miriam Buether**
Costumes	**Nicky Gillibrand**
Light	**Mimi Jordan Sherin**
Sound & Music	**David Sawer**
Casting	**Julia Horan CDG**

Hair & Make-Up Design	**Campbell Young**
Associate Sound Design	**Dominic Bilkey**
Voice	**Barbara Houseman**
Fight	**Bret Yount**
Literal Translation	**Charlotte Barslund**
Design Associate	**Lucy Sierra**
Assistant Director	**Laura Farnworth**
Trainee Assistant Director	**Roy Weise**
Stage Manager	**Joni Carter**
Deputy Stage Manager	**Lorna Seymour**
Assistant Stage Manager	**Tabitha Spence**
Costume Supervisor	**Claire Murphy**
Assistant Costume Supervisor	**Hannah Bell**
Accordion	**Ian Watson**
Set Built by	**Coventry Belgrade Production Services**
Sound Operator	**Amy Bramma**
Stage Crew	**Tom Nutt**
Wardrobe Assistant & Dresser	**Matthew Halushka**
Wigs & Hair Dresser	**Mags Pattinson**
Wardrobe Maintenance & Laundry	**Lauren Collins**
Stage Management work placement	**Zoe Dowler**

Public Enemy is generously supported by the Royal Norwegian Embassy.

Laura Farnworth is supported through the Jerwood Assistant Directors Programme at the Young Vic.

Roy Weise is supported through the Boris Karloff Trainee Assistant Directors Programme at the Young Vic.

Thanks to Nathan Osgood, Maja Eline Larssen, Kjetil Falkum, Milan Direct, Factory Settings, Andy Hilton, Tim Murley, Peter Wilkinson, Les Allitt at Iberian Lighting, Adam Norton, English Touring Theatre, Oxfam Books, George Orange at Clockwork Scenery, Mr Jorn Jacobsen MSC and Matthew Kodicek.

BIOGRAPHIES

Henrik Ibsen

One of the greatest and certainly the most influential playwrights of the 19th century, Henrik Ibsen was born in 1828 in Norway. After a number of verse plays, including *Brand* and *Peer Gynt*, he wrote the 12 monumental prose plays which are performed in every major theatre throughout the world. *Ghosts* (1881) was banned and attacked when it was first published. *Public Enemy* (1882) was Ibsen's powerfully ironic response. It's the closest to a comedy among his mature plays. Among his other modernist masterpieces are *A Doll's House* (1879), *Hedda Gabler* (1890) and *The Master Builder* (1892).

David Harrower

David Harrower's plays include *Knives in Hens, Kill the Old, Torture Their Young* and *Dark Earth* (Traverse), *Presence* (Royal Court) *The Chrysalids* (NT Connections), *Blackbird* (Edinburgh International Festival; West End; Olivier Award Best Play 2007), *A Slow Air* (Tron Theatre, Glasgow and Tricycle, London) and *Good with People* (Play,Pie and a Pint). Adaptations include Büchner's *Woyzeck* (Edinburgh Lyceum), Pirandello's *Six Characters in Search of an Author* (Young Vic), Chekhov's *Ivanov* and Horváth's *Tales from the Vienna Woods* (National Theatre), Schiller's *Mary Stuart* (National Theatre of Scotland), and Brecht's *The Good Soul of Szechuan* and Gogol's *The Government Inspector* (Young Vic).

Richard Jones Direction

Theatre work includes productions for the Old Vic, Young Vic, RSC, National Theatre, the Royal Court in the West End, and numerous productions on Broadway.

Richard has directed opera for the Royal Opera House, Glyndebourne, ENO, WNO, Opera North, Scottish Opera and in Amsterdam, Berlin, Bregenz, Brussels, Chicago, Milan, Munich, Hamburg, New York and Paris.

At the Young Vic: *Six Characters Looking For An Author, Hobson's Choice, The Good Soul Of Szechuan, Annie Get Your Gun, The Government Inspector.*

Awards include: *Into the Woods* (Olivier and Evening Standard Awards); *Der Ring Des Nibelungen* (Royal Opera House) Outstanding Artistic Achievement Award – Evening Standard; *Too Clever by Half* (Old Vic) - Olivier Award; *The Illusion* (Old Vic) – Director of the Year – Evening Standard; *Die Meistersinger Von Nurnberg* (WNO) – South Bank Sky Arts Award; *Lady Macbeth of Mtsensk* (Royal Opera House) – Olivier Award; *The Trojans* (ENO) – Olivier Award; *Hansel and Gretel* (WNO) – Olivier Award.

Miriam Buether Design

Previous Young Vic: *Wild Swans* (2013 Olivier Award Nomination, 2012 Evening Standard Award Nomination, 2012 Critics' Circle Award), *The Government Inspector, In the Red and Brown Water* (2008 Evening Standard Award Nomination), *The Good Soul Of Szechuan, generations.*

Theatre includes: *Chariots of Fire* (Hampstead, West End); *King Lear* (Public Theater); *Decade* (St Katherine's Dock, Headlong); *Earthquakes in London* (2010 Evening Standard Award), *The Effect* (National); *Sucker Punch* (2010 Evening Standard Award), *In The Republic of Happiness, Love and Information, Cock* (Royal Court); *Judgement Day* (Almeida); *Six Characters in Search of an Author* (Chichester, West End); *Guantanamo: Honor Bound to Defend Freedom* (Tricycle, West End, New York and San Francisco).

Opera includes: *Anna Nicole, Il Trittico / Suor Angelica* (Royal Opera House).

Additional awards include: 2008 Hospital Club Creative Award for Theatre; Overall winner of The Linbury Prize for Stage Design in 1999.

Born in Germany, Miriam trained at Central Saint Martin's College of Art and Design at the Akademie für Kostüm Design in Hamburg.

Nicky Gillibrand Costumes

Previous Young Vic: *Hamlet, The Government Inspector, Annie Get Your Gun, The Good Soul of Szechuan, Vernon God Little, King Lear.*

Theatre includes: *In Basildon* (Royal Court); *Billy Elliot* (West End, Broadway, Chicago, Australia); *The Tempest, Midsummer Night's Dream* (RSC); *The Seagull, Tales from the Vienna Woods* (National).

Opera includes: *Anna Nicole, Il Trittico, L'Heure Espagnole/Gianni Schicchi, Lady Macbeth of Mtsensk* (Royal Opera House); *Die Zauberflote* (Amsterdam); *Midsummer Marriage* (Munich); *Miserly Knight, Gianni Schicchi* and *Flight* (Glyndebourne); *War and Peace* (Paris); *Cavalleria Rusticana/Pagliacci, Pelléas and Mélisande, Don Giovanni* (ENO).

Awards include: the Gold award for Best Costume Design, Prague Quadrenale 2003 for *Midsummer Night's Dream* for the Royal Shakespeare Company.

Mimi Jordan Sherin Light

Previous Young Vic: *The Government Inspector, Annie Get Your Gun.*

Opera includes: ROH, Glyndebourne, The MET, ENO, WNO, La Scala, La Fenice, Bayerische Staatsoper, Wien Staatsoper, New Tokyo Opera, Chicago Lyric, Houston Grand, Royal Danish, Zurich, Lisbon, Brussels, Bregenz Opera Australia, Washington, Santa Fe and many others.

Awards: American Theatre Wing, 2 Obies, the Eddy, Tony nomination and 5 Drama Desk nominations.

In London Mimi has also worked at the Royal Court, the National, RSC and in the West End. Her American theatre work includes designs for Broadway and multiple regional theatres.

David Sawer Sound & Music

Previous Young Vic: *The Government Inspector, The Good Soul of Szechuan.*

Works include: *Flesh and Blood* (BBCSO); *Rumpelstiltskin* (BCMG); *Skin Deep* (Opera North/Bregenz Festival/Royal Danish Opera, Copenhagen); *Piano Concerto* (BBC Proms) British Composer Award 2002; *Byrnan Wood* (BBC Proms); *Rebus* (musikFabrik); *From Morning to Midnight* (English National Opera); *Tiroirs* (London Sinfonietta); *the greatest happiness principle* (BBCNOW); *Trumpet Concerto* (BBCSO); *Songs of Love and War* (BBC Singers); *Hollywood Extra* (Matrix Ensemble); *Cat's-eye*(Lontano/Ballet Rambert).

Theatre includes: *Hamlet* (RSC); *The Blue Ball* (National); *Food of Love* (Almeida); *Jackets* (Bush).

Radio includes: *Swansong* (Sony Radio Award); *The Long Time Ago Story* (BBC Radio 3).

Julia Horan CDG Casting

Previous Young Vic: *A Doll's House, Blackta, The Shawl, Wild Swans* (Young Vic/ART/ATC), *After Miss Julie, The Government Inspector, My Dad's a Birdman, Joe Turner's Come And Gone, The Glass Menagerie, Annie Get Your Gun, In The Red & Brown Water, The Good Soul Of Szechuan.*

Theatre includes: *South Downs/The Browning Version* (Harold Pinter Theatre/ Chichester Festival Theatre); *Clybourne Park* (Royal Court/Wyndhams); *Wastwater, The Heretic, Get Santa, Kin, Red Bud, Tribes, Wanderlust, Spur Of The Moment, Sucker Punch, Ingredient X* (Royal Court); *The Golden Dragon* (ATC); *Chimerica, Before the Party, The Turn of the Screw, King Lear, Children's Children, Filumena, The Knot Of The Heart; Through A Glass Darkly, Measure For Measure, When The Rain Stops Falling, In A Dark Dark House, The Homecoming* (Almeida).

Campbell Young Hair & Make-Up Design

Previous Young Vic: *A Doll's House, Three Sisters, Wild Swans, Hamlet, The Government Inspector, Annie Get Your Gun, The Good Soul of Szechuan, Vernon God Little, Six Characters Looking for an Author.*

Other theatre includes: *Ghost the Musical, Private Lives, Spider-Man, La Bête, Mary Stuart, Rock 'n' Roll, Sweeney Todd, Ghost, Betrayal, Million Dollar Quartet, The Children's Hour, La Bête, Love Never Dies, Breakfast at Tiffany's, Priscilla, Oliver, Billy Elliot, An Inspector Calls* (Broadway); *Les Misérables* (US tour).

Charlotte Barslund Literal Translation

Charlotte translates Scandinavian plays and novels.

Her translation of Strindberg's *The Pelican* was broadcast on BBC Radio 3. She translated Ingmar Bergman's version of *Ghosts* by Henrik Ibsen, which was performed at the Barbican. Her translation of the Norwegian crime novel *Calling*

Out For You! by Karin Fossum was nominated for the 2005 Gold Dagger Award by the British Crime Writers' Association.

Other translated novels include: *A Fairy Tale* by Jonas T. Bengtsson, *Dinosaur Feather* by Sissel-Jo Gazan, *When the Dead Awaken* by Steffen Jacobsen, *Machine* and *The Brummstein* by Peter Adolphsen and *Pierced* and *Burned* by Thomas Enger.

Lucy Sierra Design Associate

As Designer: *The Bear* (Improbable); *If You Don't Let Us Dream, We Wont Let You Sleep* (Royal Court); *Sweeney Todd, David Copperfield, White Nights* (Octagon Bolton); *Songs Inside* (Gate); *The Guests* (Etcetera); *Grimethorpe Race* (Arcola); *Fewer Emergencies* (Oxford Playhouse); *Symmetry, Cahoots Macbeth* (Southwark Playhouse); *The Tempest* (BBC & Barbican); *Into The Woods* (Greenwich); *Blue Funk* (Old Red Lion).

As Associate: *In The Republic of Happiness* (Royal Court); *Earthquakes In London* (Headlong/NT Tour).

Laura Farnworth Assistant Director

Laura Farnworth is Artistic Director of Undercurrent.

As Director: *Our Style is Legendary* (Tristan Bates, Nottingham Playhouse); *Dying* (in development - The Gate); *A Little Music* (Tristan Bates); *Flygirl* (National Studio); *Floor 44* (ATC/Young Vic); *Trickster* (ATC/Young Vic); *Jungle* (BAC, CPT, Ustinov Studio Bath); *The King of Schnorrers* (CPT). Laura won the NSDF Award for Storytelling and attended the National Studio Directors Course 2007.

As Assistant Director: *My City* (Almeida); *Happy Now* (National); *Paper Promises* (Young Vic); *Moon on a Rainbow Shawl* (reading Royal Court).

Laura is supported through the Jerwood Assistant Directors Programme at the Young Vic.

JERWOOD **CHARITABLE** FOUNDATION

Roy Weise Trainee Assistant Director

Roy graduated from the BA Hons Directing course at Rose Bruford College in 2011. Since graduating he has directed *SKEEN!* at Oval House Theatre and achieved his first television credit as Trainee Director on Channel 4 Random Acts film *INVISIBLE* whilst Associate Director at The Red Room Theatre & Film Company. He recently assisted Michael Buffong on *The Serpent's Tooth* (A Talawa & Almeida co-production).

Roy is supported through the Boris Karloff Trainee Assistant Directors Programme at the Young Vic.

Niall Ashdown Aslaksen

Previous Young Vic: *Annie Get Your Gun.*

Theatre includes: *Comedy Store Players* (Comedy Store); *Impropera* (Kings Place); *Accidental Death of an Anarchist* (Bolton Octagon).

Lifegame (improbable); *Hungarian Bird Festival* (UK tour).

Television includes: *Whose Line Is It Anyway, Outnumbered, Parents, Angel Cake.*

Radio includes: *The Long Count, Occupied, Losers, Hungarian Birdsong, Tunnel Vision, The Treatment.*

Adam Best Horster

Theatre includes: *Woman in Black* (West End); *Our Country's Good, Journey's End* (Original Theatre Company); *The Golden Dragon* (ATC); *Pieces of Vincent* (Arcola); *Northern Star* (Finborough); *By the Bog of Cats* (Wyndhams).

Film and television includes: *Holby City, Waking the Dead, Silent Witness, The Bill, The Catherine Tate Show, Blooded, CupCake.*

Bryan Dick Hovstad

Previous Young Vic: *Kursk.*

Theatre includes: *The Alchemist, The Life of Galileo* (National); *Amadeus* (Sheffield Crucible).

Film includes: *Master and Commander, Brothers of the Head.*

Television includes: *20,000 streets under the sky, Bleak House, Being Human, The Long Firm, Blackpool, Excluded, All The Small Things, Eric and Ernie.*

Darrell D'Silva Mayor

Previous Young Vic: *Six Characters Looking for an Author.*

Theatre includes: *Camino Real, Antony and Cleopatra, Julius Caesar, The Winter's Tale, The Drunks, Little Eagles, King Lear, The Spanish Tragedy* (RSC); *The Rose Tattoo, Closer, Further than the Furthest Thing* (National); *Hedda Gabler* (Old Vic); *Absolutely (Perhaps!)* (Wyndhams); *Antarctica* (Savoy).

Film includes: *Montana, Closer to the Moon, Jimmy's End, Dirty Pretty Things.*

Television includes: *Spooks, Criminal Justice, Krakatoa: The Final Days, Top Boy.*

Nick Fletcher Stockmann

Previous Young Vic: *A Doll's House, The Shawl.*

Theatre includes: *The Country Wife* (Royal Exchange); *A Woman Killed With Kindness, The White Guard, The Overwhelming, Once In A Lifetime, Playing With Fire, The UN Inspector* (National); *Twisted Tales* (Lyric Hammersmith); *Dial M For Murder* (West Yorkshire Playhouse); *Thyestes* (Arcola); *A Midsummer Night's Dream, The Two Gentlemen Of Verona* (Regent's Park); *King Lear* (Old Vic); *Star Quality* (Apollo); *Love's Labours Lost* (ETT); *All's Well That Ends Well* (Chicago Shakespeare Theater); *The Way Of The World* (Orange Tree); *Henry V, A Chaste Maid In Cheapside* (Shakespeare's Globe); *Burdalane* (BAC).

Television includes: *Silk, Harley Street, Midsomer Murders, New Tricks, True Dare Kiss, After The War.*

Joel Fry Billing

Theatre includes: *Wuthering Heights* (York Theatre Royal); *As You Like It* (New Vic).

Film includes: *Svengali, Tamara Drewe, 10,000 BC, A Distant Mirage, Dog Boy.*

Television includes: *Plebs, Trollied, Twenty Twelve, White Van Man, Public Enemies, Bedlam.*

Charlotte Randle Mrs Stockmann

Previous Young Vic: *King Lear.*

Theatre includes: *The King's Speech* (West End); *Decade* (Headlong); *Lingua Franca* (Finborough/59E59 New York); *Love the Sinner, Mother Courage and her Children, Romeo and Juliet* (National); *All About My Mother* (Old Vic); *Lobby Hero* (Donmar Warehouse/West End); *Don Carlos* (West End); *Rabbit* (Old Red Lion/ West End/59E59 New York); *The Dispute* (RSC).

Film and television includes: *The Brides in Bath, Dangerous Beauty.*

Radio includes: *The Other Man.*

David Sibley Morten Kiil

Previous Young Vic: *Sweet Nothings, Uncle Vanya, Cruel and Tender.*

Theatre includes: *Dallas Sweetman* (Paines Plough/Canterbury cathedral); *Space Project* (RSC/Davidson US); *Naked* (Almeida); *Dirty Wonderland* (Frantic Assembly); Edward Bond's *Lear* (Sheffield Crucible).

Film includes: *Mr Nice, Closed.*

Television includes: *Broadchurch, Utopia, Mrs Biggs, New Tricks, Wallander.*

Beatrice Walker Petra

This is Beatrice's professional debut after training at Guildhall.

Theatre in training includes: *Les Liaisons Dangereuses, The Woman* (Guildhall); *Three Sisters, Romeo and Juliet, The Seagull* (Cambridge University); *Tory Boyz, Much Ado About Nothing* (National Youth Theatre).

Reece Donn Elif

Reece Donn is 11 years old and attends the Academy Performing Arts School.

Television and film includes: Young Nipper in the feature film of Michael Morpurgo's *Private Peaceful, Charlie,* the shorts *Black Dust* and *The Dog and The Palace,* commercials for KFC, Sainsburys and opposite David Tennant in a series of idents for BBC Sports Relief.

Domenico Frescofiore Elif

Domenico is 11 years old. He took part in a BBC internal film & he was a body double in *Silent Witness* drama.

Domenico attends Sylvia Young theatre school on Saturdays and is also passionate about languages. He speaks Russian & Italian at mother tongue level as well as fluent French and beginner Mandarin. He also loves football.

Sasha Gray Morten

Sasha is 10 years old and attends the Redroofs Theatre School.

Sasha is keen on dancing, acting and singing, and he also enjoys sports, playing the piano and speaks Slovene. Sasha has previously appeared in commercials for Sony and Tesco.

Kai Hill Morten

Kai attends Redroofs Theatre School full time and loves acting, singing, street dance, rapping, playing his guitar and flying in pantomimes!

Credits include Michael Darling in *Peter Pan* at Wimbledon and Woking Theatres where he flew!

He has appeared in a Heinz commercial, voice overs and Paralymics ident and danced with *Diversity* for Disney XD channel.

Young Vic

Our shows

We present the widest variety of classics, new plays, forgotten works and music theatre. We tour and co-produce extensively within the UK and internationally.

Our artists

Our shows are created by some of the world's great theatre people alongside the most adventurous of the younger generation. This fusion makes the Young Vic one of the most exciting theatres in the world.

Our audience

. . . is famously the youngest and most diverse in London. We encourage those who don't think theatre is 'for them' to make it part of their lives. We give 10% of our tickets to schools and neighbours irrespective of box office demand, and keep prices low.

Our partners near at hand

Each year we engage with 10,000 local people – individuals and groups of all kinds including schools and colleges – by exploring theatre on and off stage. From time to time we invite our neighbours to appear on our stage alongside professionals.

Our partners further away

By co-producing with leading theatre, opera, and dance companies from around the world we create shows neither partner could achieve alone.

The Cut Bar and Restaurant

Our bar and restaurant is a relaxing place to meet and eat. An inspired mix of classic and original play-themed dishes made from fresh, free-range and organic ingredients creates an exciting menu. www.thecutbar.com

The Young Vic is a company limited by guarantee, registered in England No. 1188209

VAT registration No. 236 673 348

The Young Vic (registered charity No 268876) received public funding from

 Lambeth

Lead sponsor of the Young Vic's funded ticket scheme

Get more from the Young Vic online

Sign up to receive email updates at youngvic.org/register

 youngvictheatre

 @youngvictheatre

 youngviclondon

youngviclondon.wordpress.com

THE YOUNG VIC

To produce our sell-out, award-winning shows and provide thousands of free activities through our Taking Part programme requires major investment. Find out how you can make a difference and get involved.

As an individual . . . become a Friend, donate to a special project, attend our unique gala events or remember the Young Vic in your will.

As a company . . . take advantage of our flexible member-ships, exciting sponsorship opportunities, corporate workshops, CSR engagement and venue hire.

As a trust or foundation . . . support our innovative and forward-thinking programmes on stage and off.

Are you interested in events . . . hire a space in our award-winning building and we can work with you to create truly memorable workshops, conferences or parties.

For more information visit

youngvic.org/support us
020 7922 2810

Registered charity No. 268876

SUPPORTING THE YOUNG VIC

The Young Vic relies on the generous support of many trusts, companies, and individuals to continue our work, on and off stage. For their recent support we thank

Public Funders
Arts Council England
British Council
Lambeth Borough Council
Southwark Council

Major Supporter
Otkritie Capital

Corporate Supporters
American Airlines
Barclays
Bloomberg
Coutts
Markit
Taylor Wessing LLP
The Cooperative

Corporate Members
aka
Bates, Wells & Braithwaite
Bloomberg
Clifford Chance
Ingenious Media Plc
Lane Consulting
Memery Crystal
Promise

Partners
Eric Abraham
Tony & Gisela Bloom
Chris & Jane Lucas
Patrick McKenna
Simon & Midge Palley
Jon & Noralee Sedmak
Justin Shinebourne
Ramez & Tiziana Sousou
The Ulrich Family
Anda & Bill Winters

Soul Mates
Royce & Rotha Bell
Beatrice Bondy
Caroline & Ian Cormack
Patrick Handley
Justin & Jill Manson
Miles Morland
Rita & Paul Skinner

Jane Attias
Chris & Ruth Baker
Rory Bateman

Chris & Frances Bates
The Bickertons
Katie Bradford
CJ & LM Braithwaite
Tim & Caroline Clark
Kay Ellen Consolver
Susan Dark
Miel de Botton
Annabel Duncan-Smith
Robyn Durie
Jennifer & Jeff Eldredge
Paul Gambaccini
Annika Goodwille
Sarah Hall
Richard Hardman & Family
Jaakko Harlas
Nik Holttum & Helen Brannigan
Maxine Isaacs
Suzanne & Michael Johnson
John Kinder & Gerry Downey
Tom Keatinge
Mr & Mrs Herbert Kretzmer
Carol Lake
Jude Law
Michael Lebovitz & Ana Paludi
Ann Lewis
Tony Mackintosh
James & Sue Macmillan
Ian McKellen
John McLaughlin
Juliet Medforth
Barbara Minto
Dounia & Sherif Nadar
Georgia Oetker
Sally O'Neill
Rob & Lesley O'Rahilly
Barbara Reeves
Anthony & Sally Salz
Charles & Donna Scott
Bhagat Sharma
Dasha Shenkman
Lois Sieff
Melissa A. Smith
Jan & Michael Topham
The Tracy Family
Donna & Richard Vinter
Jimmy & Carol Walker
Rob Wallace
Edgar & Judith Wallner
George & Patricia White
Mrs Fiona Williams

Trust Supporters
29th May 1961 Charitable Trust
95.8 Capital FM's Help a Capital Child
BBC Children in Need
Boris Karloff Foundation
The Boshier-Hinton Foundation
The City Bridge Trust
John S Cohen Foundation
D'Oyly Carte Charitable Trust
Equitable Charitable Trust
Esmée Fairbairn Foundation
Garfield Weston Foundation
Genesis Foundation
Golden Bottle Trust
Gosling Foundation
Harold Hyam Wingate Foundation
Henry Smith Charity
Jerwood Charitable Foundation
John Ellerman Foundation
John Thaw Foundation
KPMG Foundation
Lambeth HAP
The Limbourne Trust
Martin Bowley Charitable Trust
Newcomen Collett Foundation
The Nomura Charitable Trust
The Portrack Charitable Trust
Progress Foundation
Red Hill Trust
Richard Radcliffe Trust
Rix Thompson Rothenberg Foundation
Royal Norwegian Embassy
The Royal Victoria Hall Foundation
Santander Foundation
SFIA Educational Trust
Sir Siegmund Warburg's Voluntary Settlement
The Steel Charitable Trust

and all other donors who wish to remain anonymous.

markit™

Markit is proud to be the Lead Sponsor of the

Young Vic's Funded Ticket Programme

Enabling theatre to be enjoyed by all

www.markit.com

Public Enemy

Henrik Ibsen (1828–1906), Norwegian poet and playwright, was one of the shapers of modern theatre, who tempered naturalism with an understanding of social responsibility and individual psychology. His earliest major plays, *Brand* (1866) and *Peer Gynt* (1867), were large-scale verse dramas, but with *Pillars of the Community* (1877) he began to explore contemporary issues. There followed *A Doll's House* (1879), *Ghosts* (1881) and *An Enemy of the People* (1882). A richer understanding of the complexity of human impulses marks such later works as *The Wild Duck* (1885), *Rosmersholm* (1886), *Hedda Gabler* (1890) and *The Master Builder* (1892), while the imminence of mortality overshadows his last great plays, *John Gabriel Borkman* (1896) and *When We Dead Awaken* (1899).

David Harrower's plays include *Knives in Hens*, *Kill the Old, Torture Their Young* and *Dark Earth* (Traverse), *Presence* (Royal Court), *The Chrysalids* (NT Connections), *Blackbird* (Edinburgh International Festival; West End; Olivier Award Best Play 2007), *A Slow Air* (Tron Theatre, Glasgow; Tricycle, London) and *Good with People* (Play, Pie and a Pint). His adaptations include Büchner's *Woyzeck* (Edinburgh Lyceum), Pirandello's *Six Characters in Search of an Author* (Young Vic), Chekhov's *Ivanov* and Horváth's *Tales from the Vienna Woods* (National Theatre), Schiller's *Mary Stuart* (National Theatre of Scotland), and Brecht's *The Good Soul of Szechuan* and Gogol's *The Government Inspector* (Young Vic).

by the same author

DARK EARTH
PRESENCE
THE CHRYSALIDS
(adapted from the novel by John Wyndham)
PURPLE
(translated from the play by Jon Fosse
and included in *Shell Connections 2003* anthology)
TALES FROM THE VIENNA WOODS (Horváth)
SWEET NOTHINGS (adapted from Schnitzler)
THE GOVERNMENT INSPECTOR (Gogol)
A SLOW AIR

Published by Methuen
KNIVES IN HENS
KILL THE OLD, TORTURE THEIR YOUNG
SIX CHARACTERS IN SEARCH OF AN AUTHOR (Pirandello)

Published by Oberon
IVANOV (Chekhov)
THE GIRL ON THE SOFA (Jon Fosse)

HENRIK IBSEN

Public Enemy

a new version by

DAVID HARROWER

from a literal translation by
Charlotte Barslund

faber and faber

First published in 2013
by Faber and Faber Limited
74–77 Great Russell Street
London WC1B 3DA

Typeset by Country Setting, Kingsdown, Kent CT14 8ES
Printed in England by CPI Group (UK) Ltd, Croydon CR0 4YY

A CIP record for this book
is available from the British Library

ISBN 978–0–571–30823–1

2 4 6 8 10 9 7 5 3 1

Public Enemy in this version was first presented at the Young Vic Theatre, London, on 4 May 2013. The cast was as follows:

Aslaksen Niall Ashdown
Horster Adam Best
Hovstad Bryan Dick
Mayor Darrell D'Silva
Stockmann Nick Fletcher
Billing Joel Fry
Mrs Stockmann Charlotte Randle
Morten Kiil David Sibley
Petra Beatrice Walker
Eilif Reece Donn, Domenico Frescofiore
Morten Sasha Gray, Kai Hill

Director Richard Jones
Designer Miriam Buether
Costumes Nicky Gillibrand
Lighting Mimi Jordan Sherin
Music and Sound David Sawer

Characters

in order of appearance

Mrs Stockmann

Billing

The Mayor
(Peter Stockmann)

Hovstad

Dr Thomas Stockmann

Horster

Petra

Eilif

Morten

Kiil

Aslaksen

Act One

Evening. The living room of Dr Thomas Stockmann's house.

  Billing sits at the dinner table, a napkin under his chin. Mrs Stockmann hands him a dish of roast beef.

Mrs Stockmann It's cold I'm afraid, but you are an hour late.

Billing No, it's delicious. *Very* good.

Mrs Stockmann Thomas is very particular about when we eat.

Billing I'm so sorry. But I'm happy here on my own. I can give this roast beef my full attention.

  A sound from the hall, off.

Mrs Stockmann That will be Mr Hovstad, will it?

Billing Should be. Even later than me.

  Enter Mayor Peter Stockmann in overcoat and official trappings.

Mayor Katrine, good evening.

Mrs Stockmann Peter, how nice to see you.

Mayor I was . . . (*Spots Billing.*) But you have company.

Mrs Stockmann (*slightly embarassed*) No, he arrived late and . . . Are you hungry? Will you have something to eat?

Mayor I don't eat after seven.

Mrs Stockmann Of course, I forgot.

Mayor I had a sandwich earlier – more than enough.

Mrs Stockmann (*smiles*) You make us feel so excessive . . .

Mayor Not a word I'd use about you, Katrine. Not you. (*Points towards study.*) Is Thomas here?

Mrs Stockmann The boys dragged him out for a walk.

Noises heard from outside.

Mayor That will be them now.

Mrs Stockmann No, I don't think so . . . (*A knock.*) Come in.

Hovstad enters.

Mr Hovstad . . .

Hovstad My apologies, I was held up at the printers. (*To the Mayor.*) Good evening.

Mayor Evening, Hovstad. What brings you here – business?

Hovstad Partly.

Mayor *The Reformer* never rests.

Hovstad Your brother's written something for us.

Mayor (*smiles*) He can't help himself, can he?

Hovstad If something important needs said, it's best said openly to encourage discussion, don't you think?

Mrs Stockmann Mr Hovstad . . .

Mayor Discussion? Your readership agrees unquestioningly with every word you publish. Every word. I'm teasing you, Hovstad, really, I have no ill feeling towards your publication.

Hovstad We must be getting something wrong then.

Mayor Your radical newspaper must concede the public mood is optimistic. There's a changed atmosphere in the town. It's been transformed.

Mrs Stockmann Yes, the miracle of the Baths.

Mayor Absolutely.

Mrs Stockmann Thomas says exactly the same.

Mayor The upturn we've seen in two short years. People have money in their pockets again; local businesses are thriving. Property values increasing. Land prices going up.

Hovstad And let's not forget people are working again.

Mayor Which in turn reduces the cost of welfare on the taxpayer. Everyone wins. Hence we must all make sure this summer is our best yet. It's certainly looking that way. Bookings are already double what they were this time last year.

Hovstad Perfect timing for the Doctor's article.

Mayor He's written about the Baths?

Hovstad Praising their health benefits. I held it back from last winter – I thought now would be the best time to print it, when people are planning their summer holidays.

Mayor Good thinking, Hovstad.

Mrs Stockmann Thomas is so proud of the Baths.

Mayor I should hope so, he is their Medical Officer.

Hovstad And their creator, let's not forget.

Mayor I like to think I also played a substantial part.

Mrs Stockmann You did, Peter. Thomas always says so.

Hovstad You brought them to fruition, I know, but the initial idea was Dr Stockmann's.

Mayor Thomas has nothing *but* ideas crammed into his head. All fine and good, but when something needs to be *done* . . . well, that takes a different kind of person.

Mrs Stockmann Of course, Peter.

Hovstad So let me get this straight . . .

Mrs Stockmann Mr Hovstad, please, some food before it gets cleared away. Thomas will be back any moment now.

Hovstad Thank you, maybe I will.

He enters the dining room.

Mayor (*voice lowered*) So crass and aggressive. Peasant.

Mrs Stockmann Peter, you know you both share the credit . . .

Mayor Thomas seems to have trouble with sharing the credit.

Mrs Stockmann You know that's nonsense. You're brothers and good friends . . . That will be him now.

Stockmann (*off, laughing*) Katrine! We have another guest. In you go.

Captain Horster enters, greets Mrs Stockmann. Following him, Dr Stockmann and his sons Eilif and Morten.

Mrs Stockmann Captain Horster.

Stockmann We met him on the street. Had to really twist his arm, didn't we, boys? (*Indicates roast beef.*) Help yourself, Captain. And these gannets, they're hungry again . . .

Horster and the boys cross to the dining table and start to help themselves.

Mrs Stockmann Thomas . . .

Stockmann (*sees his brother*) Hello, Peter! Boys, it's Uncle Peter. You'll have to fight them for the roast beef, Captain!

He shakes Peter's hand.

Sit yourself down.

Mayor No. I can't, thank you.

Stockmann (*opening wine*) Why not? Relax, put your feet up.

Mayor I'm not a great drinker, you know that.

Stockmann You don't have to be great, you can just be so-so.

Mayor I'm not one for drinking parties either.

Stockmann This isn't a drinking party.

Mayor (*looks towards dining room*) Your boys eat like horses.

Stockmann They're young. Nothing wrong with healthy appetites. They need strength; strong arms to grab the world and give it a good shake.

Mayor I didn't realise it needed shaking.

Stockmann Ask them in a few years' time when they're men – I'm sure they'll be quick to tell us what we got wrong. Two old fogeys like you and me, we can't see it.

Mayor One, I am not an old fogey. Two, my eyesight is fine, thank you.

Stockmann I get delirious being around them. Their gusto for life. What they've yet to see and discover and learn. They *infect* me. It's like a new world revealing itself.

Mayor Sounds exhausting.

Stockmann You don't see it, Peter, because you've always lived here. The shine's rubbed off. Remember, up north, we were cut off from everything. And the God-awful people who lived there . . . Dead. Unstimulating. Returning here has been . . . It's a small town but it feels like a metropolis.

Mayor I hope we never become that.

Stockmann Life is here. Energy. Things to get involved in and work towards. (*Breaks off. Shouts.*) Katrine? Was there any post today? Anything for me?

Mrs Stockmann No, nothing's come.

Stockmann (*indicates food table and guests*) And all this . . . The good things. Life as it should be lived. Less than a year ago we were starving, we could never have imagined this. Roast beef for dinner. And warmth. And company. Try some. It's sublime.

Mayor Katrine's already tried tempting me.

Stockmann Did you see the new lampshade she bought?

Mayor Yes, I noticed it.

Stockmann Stand here. No, here. It casts its light downwards. Makes the room so comfortable. Elegant, don't you think?

Mayor Elegant, yes. Expensive, I'm sure.

Stockmann We can allow ourselves certain luxuries now. Katrine says that I earn almost as much as she spends. I work hard; I think we deserve it. I'm sure the town magistrate isn't averse to the good things in life.

Mayor He can afford them, he's a magistrate, a very senior public official.

Stockmann A tradesman then, he'll spend . . . We are not profligate, as I think you're trying to insinuate.

Mayor Did I say a word?

Stockmann And it's certainly not money wasted. Look. People enjoying themselves, enjoying our food. I need this. Surrounded by young, forward-thinking people who have opinions and minds of their own . . . You should talk to Hovstad, you might come to like him.

Mayor He's running a piece you've written about the Baths.

Stockmann Is he? No, no, that can't be published.

Mayor As he said, spring is the perfect time.

Stockmann Ordinarily.

Mayor What do you mean by that?

Stockmann I can't say.

Mayor Thomas . . .

Stockmann I can't. Not at the moment. It may be nothing. My imagination.

Mayor I am Chairman of the Baths Committee.

Stockmann I'm well aware of that.

Mayor It is your duty to inform me.

Stockmann I will inform you when I'm –

Mayor No, you will do it *now*!

Stockmann We should both calm down.

Mayor I am perfectly calm. And I am saying to you that everything must go through official channels. We can't tolerate secrecy or anything underhand . . .

Stockmann When have I ever been secretive or underhand?

Mayor You've always gone your own way. And in a well-ordered community, we cannot have people who do that. You must learn to conform and accept the decisions made by the elected authorities – decisions made for the *common* good.

Stockmann Well, that's debatable. I still fail to see how this concerns me.

Mayor You see . . .! Precisely my point. You think you stand apart. Well, I'd be careful because sooner or later, it could backfire on you.

Stockmann You've got this completely wrong!

Mayor I am rarely wrong, Thomas. And I'm tired of . . .

He breaks off, turns and walks out. Mrs Stockmann enters.

Mrs Stockmann What was that about?

Stockmann How can I tell him about something I'm not even sure about myself?

Mrs Stockmann What are you not sure about?

Stockmann It doesn't matter. Did that postman bring *nothing*?

Hovstad, Billing and Horster enter the living room and sit around the table.

Billing That was delicious.

Hovstad Do we give the Mayor indigestion, I wonder?

Stockmann He needs to have control over everything.

Hovstad He wants the *Reformer* obliterated, not controlled.

Stockmann He's lonely. He has no private life, no home comforts. That's why he fills his time with meetings and committees, pouring endless cups of tea into himself. (*Goes for bottle of wine.*) Who's for another? Cigars, Eilif. Morten, get my pipe, will you?

The boys go to fetch them.

(*To Horster.*) Come and sit beside me, stranger, tell me about life at sea.

The boys re-enter.

Here we are. (*To Morten.*) How many puffs did you take? . . . Offer them round, Eilif.

Mrs Stockmann Where do you sail to next, Captain Horster?

Horster America, in a week's time.

Billing So you'll miss the council election?

Horster There's an election?

Billing You must know that!

Horster I don't pay attention to politics.

Billing People who don't vote should be arrested and charged with evasion of duty.

Horster I don't understand what any of the parties are talking about.

Billing Then try to. Democracy was fought for tooth and nail.

Horster I'm so ignorant I wouldn't know what I'm voting for.

Billing Imagine your ship was society. You don't think everyone on board should have a say where it's going?

Horster It would hit the rocks almost immediately.

Hovstad Sailors only care about the weather. And rum.

Billing I just don't understand your attitude at all.

Hovstad Save your energy.

Stockmann Sailors are like migratory birds – equally at home in the north or the south. All the more reason for us to be even more active, Mr Hovstad. I meant to say, the piece I wrote . . .

Hovstad Yes, we have room for it so we're using it tomorrow . . .

Stockmann You can't. I don't want it published.

Hovstad Why not?

Stockmann I would rather you didn't. Not yet.

Petra enters, carrying exercise books.

Petra Good evening, gentlemen. All sitting comfortably, I see, whilst I've been out slaving.

Stockmann Petra, have a seat. Join us.

Billing What's it to be?

Petra I'll pour it. You always make it too strong. Mm, Dad, I have a letter for you.

Stockmann Give me it! You've had it on you all day?

Petra (*hands it to him*) The postman gave me it this morning but I was rushing to school . . .

Stockmann This is it! This is what I've been waiting for. Excuse me for a moment, I have to . . .

He hurries into his study.

Petra What is it?

Mrs Stockmann I've no idea. He's been pestering the postman for days.

Billing One of his patients maybe?

Petra Poor Dad works too hard. (*Drinks.*) That's better.

Hovstad Where have you been slaving this evening?

Petra Evening class.

Billing After teaching all day . . . You're a shining example to us all.

Mrs Stockmann And now she'll spend her whole evening correcting homework.

Petra No one else is going to do it.

Hovstad Do you never stop?

Petra I don't mind. I get tired but it's a good tiredness.

Billing She likes feeling tired . . .!

Petra I sleep better.

Morten You're a sinner, Petra.

Petra Am I now? How do you work that out?

Morten Mr Rorlund says that work's a punishment for our sins.

Eilif He's stupid, believing something stupid like that.

Mrs Stockmann Eilif . . .

Billing Let him speak.

Hovstad Is your ambition never to work hard then? What do you plan to do with your life?

Morten I want to be a Viking.

Eilif That means you'll be a heathen.

Morten So I'll be a heathen.

Billing Damn it, we should all be heathens. Burn down everything we see. Everything that gets in –

Mrs Stockmann Mr Billing . . .

Morten You can do whatever you want if you're a heathen!

Billing Well, perhaps not . . .

Mrs Stockmann (*interrupts*) Through now, boys, you've homework to finish.

The boys leave.

Hovstad Talk like that won't harm them.

Mrs Stockmann I would rather they didn't hear it.

Petra You don't want them to hear anything.

Mrs Stockmann Certain things, no, not at home.

Petra What kind of children are we raising? We tell them lies at school and cover their ears at home.

Horster You lie at school?

Petra I'm forced to teach the children things I don't believe in.

Billing I don't know how you can stand it.

Petra If I had the money I'd start my own school. Teach what *I* think should be taught.

Billing Ah, money . . . I'd give you some if I had any.

Horster You'd be welcome to use a room in my house.

Petra Thank you, but I don't think the town's ready for it.

Hovstad You're wasted on children – Petra's future is journalism.

Mrs Stockmann What do you mean?

Hovstad I've asked her to translate an American story for us. The deadline's fast approaching, Petra.

Petra I'll have it done, don't worry.

Stockmann returns, brandishing the letter.

Mrs Stockmann Are you going to reveal the great mystery?

Stockmann Rocks.

Hovstad What?

Stockmann Captain Horster, we've hit the rocks.

Mrs Stockmann What do you mean?

Stockmann I was right. Absolutely spot on. They think I'm a crackpot but wait until they read this. I want to see their faces then.

Petra Tell us, Dad . . .

Stockmann I will. I wish my brother was here. This proves how wrong he is – how . . . blind. We promote ourselves as the healthiest town in the region, don't we?

Hovstad Yes, we do.

Stockmann If you're weak or ill – even if you're fighting fit – come and restore yourself; relax, recuperate. Let our spa waters transform you.

Mrs Stockmann Thomas, what . . .

Stockmann I've done it too – I've been part of it. Writing about the Baths, praising them to the skies.

Billing I described them once as 'the beating heart of the town'.

Stockmann You know what they really are? Our marvellous, renowned Baths – do you know what they really are?

Hovstad What?

Mrs Stockmann Tell us.

Stockmann A poisonous cesspit.

Petra The Baths?

21

Stockmann They're lethal. Toxic.

Billing I don't understand . . .

Hovstad *Toxic?*

Stockmann Ridden with bacteria. We have on our hands a catastrophe – a public health risk of the highest order. You know the swamp up in Molledalen near the tanneries – the one that smells so revolting? The filth from that has seeped into the water table.

Hovstad I don't understand.

Stockmann That water is pumped from the pump-room down pipes and out on to the beach.

Hovstad The beach where the Baths are?

Stockmann Exactly.

Hovstad You're sure?

Stockmann Now I am, absolutely. There were a number of unusual illnesses among our visitors last year. Typhus, gastric problems . . .

Mrs Stockmann Yes, I remember.

Stockmann We thought they brought those complaints with them but I was never one-hundred-per-cent convinced. So I made some tests of the water.

Mrs Stockmann That's what you've been so busy with.

Stockmann I had them sent to the university laboratory to be properly analysed.

Hovstad And those are the results?

Stockmann (*reads*) '. . . We therefore conclude that exposure to the water both internally and externally will cause serious and lasting damage to health.' You see? No one must swim in it, no one must swallow it.

Mrs Stockmann My brilliant doctor. Thank goodness you found out in time.

Hovstad So, what now?

Stockmann What do you mean, what now? It has to be put right.

Hovstad But how?

Stockmann There's a way. There's a solution. But we have to act quickly or the Baths are – We'll have to shut them down for good.

Mrs Stockmann You've kept this so secret.

Stockmann I should have gone around town declaring it?

Petra You could have told *us*.

Stockmann Not until I had proof. First thing tomorrow, Petra, I want you to bring the Skunk here –

Mrs Stockmann Thomas . . .

Stockmann – bring your grandfather here. He thinks I'm certifiable like the rest of them. Well, now they'll have to sit up and listen. This will cause an uproar. The whole system has to be dug up and relaid.

Hovstad *All* of it?

Stockmann We have no alternative. The water intake is too low – it has to be moved higher up the hill.

Petra So you were right, Dad.

Stockmann Petra remembers. I wrote to the committee before building started and warned them about this. Not one of them replied. Too caught up in the excitement. (*Holds up papers.*) This is the report I've written – four pages of evidence and this (*the letter*) makes it irrefutable. I need something to put it in. Good, now, give it to . . .

(*Stamps his foot.*) What the hell's her name? The girl.
Give it to her, tell her to deliver it to Peter right away.

Mrs Stockmann exits with the letter.

Petra Can you imagine Uncle Peter's face . . .

Stockmann There's nothing he can object to. It's all there
in black and white.

Hovstad Can I run a short piece on this? Better sooner
than later.

Stockmann Yes, yes I suppose you're right.

Mrs Stockmann (*enters*) She's taken it.

Billing You'll be celebrated as our saviour, Dr Stockmann.

Stockmann I'm only doing my duty. And it was . . .

Billing We'll have a dinner in your honour!

Hovstad There should be a vote of thanks. The Town
Council should honour you.

Stockmann No, I want nothing like that, thank you.

Petra What about a pay rise?

Stockmann No. I wouldn't take it. I wouldn't, Katrine.

Mrs Stockmann We can talk about that . . .

Stockmann The respect of people I respect is enough.

Petra To my far-sighted father!

Others Cheers.

Horster To your discovery. I wish you only the best.

Stockmann Thank you, thank you, my friends, thank
you. This is for my home town. The town I love.

Act Two

Morning. Stockmann's living room. Mrs Stockmann hands her husband a sealed letter.

Mrs Stockmann It's from Peter . . .

Stockmann Ah. (*Opens, reads.*) 'I am hereby returning the report you submitted . . .' (*Reads on to himself.*) Hmm . . .

Mrs Stockmann What does he say?

Stockmann He's coming here at twelve. Nothing else.

Mrs Stockmann But you have patients to see.

Stockmann I've finished my morning calls.

Mrs Stockmann I wonder how he's taken it?

Stockmann Not well, I imagine. I made the discovery, not him. I may get a begrudging thank you at some point in the future.

Mrs Stockmann You could be generous and say it was Peter who drew your attention to it.

Stockmann Yes, it doesn't matter to me. As long as it's put right.

Morten Kiil appears, laughing to himself.

Kiil Is it true, what I'm hearing?

Mrs Stockmann Daddy, come in . . .

Stockmann Good morning, Morten.

Kiil Is it? Is it true? If not, I'm not staying.

Stockmann Yes, it's true.

Kiil The water's going to kill us all?

Stockmann Who have you been talking to?

Kiil Petra. It really *is* true? Really? It's not an April fool? You're not trying to trick me? Look at me, Stockmann . . . It's not true, is it?

Stockmann It is true. And we're very lucky . . .

Kiil (*laughs*) Lucky? Now, you're really having me on . . .

Stockmann Lucky that it's been discovered before the Baths open for the summer . . .

Kiil You're provoking him, aren't you? You're deliberately provoking Peter.

Mrs Stockmann No, Daddy, Thomas is not provoking him.

Kiil Lots of tiny animals crawling in the water?

Stockmann Bacteria.

Mrs Stockmann Probably hundreds of thousands of them.

Kiil But no one can see them, is that right?

Stockmann Invisible to the naked eye.

Kiil And you think the Mayor will fall for that?

Stockmann He has to.

Kiil If he's gullible enough.

Stockmann Let's hope the whole town's gullible enough.

Kiil I hope they all fall for it – every one of those back-stabbing bastards. I want them kicked out just like they kicked me out. Grab their balls, Thomas –

Mrs Stockmann Daddy . . .

Kiil – and squeeze them hard. I want to hear them squeal. I'll donate a hundred to charity if I can hear them from my tannery.

Stockmann You heard that, Katrine.

Kiil Maybe not a hundred. Fifty. At Christmas.

Hovstad enters.

Hovstad Morning. Door was open. Am I . . . ?

Stockmann No, come in.

Kiil So you're in on this too?

Hovstad In on what?

Stockmann Yes, he is.

Kiil It'll be in the newspaper? (*Roars with laughter.*)

Hovstad I just need a few minutes.

Kiil Of course. Squeeze, Thomas. Squeeze their balls and then twist. I want to hear them scream.

He exits with Mrs Stockmann.

Hovstad Heard anything?

Stockmann No. But Peter's on his way here.

Hovstad I've been thinking about this all night. You're a doctor – a scientist – and for you this is an isolated case. I don't think you realise this is connected to many other things.

Stockmann I don't follow.

Hovstad The impurities in the soil have polluted the water supply, yes?

Stockmann Yes. And the impurity is directly linked to the Molledalen swamp.

Hovstad Ah, but there's another swamp.

Stockmann Another swamp? Where?

Hovstad The communal swamp we've sunk into. The swelling army of bureaucrats and pen-pushers who are choking us to death. Whilst the rich who have the real power sit in their huge houses counting their fortunes and laughing at how easy it is to control us.

Stockmann Come on, that's going too far.

Hovstad Is it? Doesn't the power of the wealthy disgust you? They stand in the way of progress and equality and enlightenment.

Stockmann Some of them are well-intentioned, intelligent people . . .

Hovstad The same well-intentioned, intelligent people who ignored your warnings about the water pipes . . . ?

Stockmann Well, they were misguided. It was rash. Now they have to rectify their mistake.

Hovstad And you're confident they will?

Stockmann Yes. I'm sure it will meet some resistance amongst the committee at first . . .

Hovstad That's when the *Reformer* can come in hard.

Stockmann That won't be necessary. I'm sure my brother . . .

Hovstad Forgive me, Doctor, but I won't let them off the hook. I want to make things uncomfortable for that bunch of self-serving parasites.

Stockmann You've tried that before, Hovstad. They almost closed you down.

Hovstad No, we backed off and . . . Simple expedience. The Baths were still being built; we didn't want to jeopardise that. But now the truce is over.

Stockmann You should still give credit where it's due.

Hovstad We will. But I will not let this opportunity pass. We must destroy this myth that our leaders are infallible. They are not.

Stockmann I agree with you up to a point.

Hovstad I know this concerns your brother and I'm sorry, but enough is enough. Truth must not be the servant of money.

Stockmann Of course, but . . .

Hovstad I come from extreme poverty, Dr Stockmann. I've seen life from the very bottom of the heap. The poor have no voice. They're excluded. The doors to the Council are kept locked and bolted. Break down those doors and they will prosper.

Stockmann I understand your anger, I do, I do. I feel much the same.

Hovstad The oppressed will be liberated. Emancipated. They'll call it rebellion, they always do, but we will be the many against the few.

A knock at the door.

Stockmann Come in.

Aslaksen enters.

Aslaksen Excuse me, Doctor, for intruding like this . . .

Stockmann Ah, Mr . . .

Aslaksen Aslaksen. The printer.

Hovstad It's me he wants.

Aslaksen No. Dr Stockmann.

Stockmann What can I do for you?

Aslaksen Mr Billing has told me you wish to see an improved water system in place, am I right?

Stockmann That is correct.

Aslaksen I've come to let you know, sir, you have my full support.

Hovstad Word's getting round . . .

Stockmann Thank you, but I . . .

Aslaksen And if it helps, other businesses too. They'll get behind you. We don't raise our voices but we can make ourselves felt. We're the majority and our support will help you.

Stockmann Look, this is a simple, straightforward matter.

Aslaksen I know the authorities, I know them well. Dealt with them for years. They don't like criticism, who does? But we must make our voices heard. A small demonstration perhaps?

Hovstad Good. That's a start.

Stockmann Demonstrate *how*?

Aslaksen Sensibly of course. It's how I find best to go about things, sir. The Baths promise great wealth for this town. This matter of the water is vital to me and to the small businessmen, who, I believe, I have a certain influence over.

Stockmann I am aware of that, Mr Aslaksen.

Aslaksen And I know they will all be very grateful for what you're doing.

Stockmann I thank you for your support. For all your support. Now, will you have a drink? Spirits or beer?

Aslaksen No, thank you. I am head of the Temperance Society.

Stockmann Of course you are.

Aslaksen Now I have to go. There's people I must talk to.

Stockmann Look, please don't waste your time. This will be resolved.

Aslaksen Authorities, Doctor – they procrastinate. I'm not criticising them, we need them, but . . .

Hovstad The editorial tomorrow will expose them . . .

Aslaksen You must be sensible, Hovstad. Sensible. Trust me, I know. The majority are with you, Doctor. Are you coming?

Hovstad In a while.

Stockmann Thank you, Mr Aslaksen.

Aslaksen Goodbye.

Aslaksen exits.

Hovstad A good man, but he's weak and spineless, petrified of upsetting anyone. Men like him can't commit to any action.

Stockmann I think he's sincere though.

Hovstad Sincere? We want people who know what must change and why. All this ridiculous bowing and kneeling before authority has to end.

Stockmann Let me to speak to my brother.

Hovstad And if he does nothing?

Stockmann He will.

Hovstad But if not?

Stockmann Print it. Print the full report.

Hovstad I have your word on that?

Stockmann Absolutely. Here, take it.

Hovstad We'll speak soon then.

Stockmann Peter will act on my report, I assure you.

Hovstad exits.

(*To the dining room.*) Katrine! . . . You're home, Petra?

Petra I've just got back.

Mrs Stockmann (*enters*) No sign of Peter?

Stockmann No, but I've had a long talk with Hovstad. He's fascinated by what I've discovered. It's more wide-ranging than I imagined, you know. He's going to help me push for the changes I want.

Mrs Stockmann Will you need him?

Stockmann I'm certain I shan't. And Aslaksen, who represents the small businesses, he's with me as well. It's building, Katrine. Gathering momentum. The majority are getting behind me.

Petra That's excellent, Dad.

Doorbell rings.

Stockmann That will be Peter. (*A knock.*) Come in.

Mayor (*enters*) Good morning.

Stockmann Morning.

Mrs Stockmann Hello, Peter. How are you?

Mayor Very well. You received the report back?

Stockmann Yes, thank you. You did read it?

Mayor I did, yes.

Stockmann And what have you to say?

The Mayor glances at the women. The women leave.

Mayor Not a word. All those tests and not a word to me.

Stockmann I needed to be certain.

Mayor And now you are?

Stockmann You've read it. Is it not obvious?

Mayor And you intend to present this to the committee as an official statement?

Stockmann That's my intention, yes.

Mayor You chose to use some very vivid wording. 'Lethal'. 'Toxic'. What else? 'Chronic poisoning'. A bit theatrical, no?

Stockmann Taken internally or exposed to bare skin, the water *is* poisonous. It is lethal. I don't use such words lightly. When I wrote it I had in my head all the poor, sick people who come here in good faith and pay us a fortune to improve their health.

Mayor And to remedy this all we have to do is simply build another sewer that will drain away the first sewer at Molledalen, yes? Then dig up and re-lay our entire water system?

Stockmann There's no other viable solution.

Mayor This morning I asked an engineer for an estimate – confidentially of course. The cost of your proposed changes? Several hundred *thousand*.

Stockmann That much?

Mayor Which would take at least two years to complete. During which the Baths would have to close – unless you imagine people would continue to come here knowing they may be 'chronically poisoned'?

Stockmann I'll say it again. That is what will happen.

Mayor This year will be our biggest so far. And, of course, neighbouring towns won't just stand by. They've seen our success. Within a year, I guarantee you, they'll have transformed themselves into bathing resorts and we will be forgotten. A ghost town. No one will ever come back to us. Your report will have ruined us.

Stockmann *Ruined?*

Mayor Did you never for a moment consider that, Thomas?

Stockmann Tell me what you think *should* be done?

Mayor After some consideration, I am not convinced it's quite as bad as you make out.

Stockmann No, it's more likely worse. Or it will be, in the summer when the weather gets warmer and the bacteria multiply.

Mayor I really do believe you've exaggerated the case. A competent doctor knows how to treat a patient's symptoms and remedy them if they become too pronounced . . .

Stockmann What are you saying?

Mayor The water system that we installed will remain where it is and will continue to serve the town. Now, it could well be in the near future, that the committee does come to an agreement that there are sufficient grounds for certain improvements.

Stockmann I don't understand how any doctor could do that. I do understand deception.

Mayor This is not deception.

Stockmann It is fraud and suppression of the truth and it shows contempt for the people who live in this community.

Mayor Thomas, how else can I put it? I am just not convinced that there is any immediate danger to public health.

Stockmann Yes, you are. My report couldn't be clearer. You are but you won't admit it. You and your committee rushed through the siting of the water pipes. No consultation whatsoever.

Mayor I govern and work for the good of this town and its people. I cannot be associated with a scandal. I won't have that. Your report will not go to the committee. It will not leave this room. I may bring the matter up at a later date.

Stockmann There are people who already know.

Mayor (*after a moment*) You've told Hovstad . . .

Stockmann Who will make sure you do your duty.

Mayor Reckless, Thomas. Stupid. Irresponsible. Do you know what the consequences of this could be? For all of you?

Stockmann The consequences?

Mayor I've been a loyal brother to you. I've helped you, supported you.

Stockmann And we are very grateful for your help.

Mayor The elected leader of the town cannot have people around him who embarrass him.

Stockmann I *embarrass* you?

Mayor Unfortunately you do. This need to pronounce on *every*thing. An idea comes into your head, out it comes in the *Reformer*.

Stockmann Because I believe the public should know what I'm thinking.

Mayor The public don't need new ideas. They do just fine with existing ones. Thomas, you're your own worst enemy. The reason people in power overlook you is because you're difficult.

Stockmann Difficult?

Mayor You only got the Medical Officer job because of me.

Stockmann It was mine by right.

Mayor That's not how others saw it.

Stockmann The Baths were my idea! I had to shout for years before anyone listened.

Mayor You wanted them built immediately. But there were procedures to go through, committees . . . You didn't help your cause one –

Stockmann None of you listened . . .!

Mayor People don't appreciate being *harangued*.

Stockmann That's why we're in this mess.

Mayor You always have to attack, attack . . .

Stockmann You're to blame, not me.

Mayor Anyone who disagrees with you is worthless. I don't know what else to say. I've told you what will happen to the town – you won't even consider it for one second.

Stockmann There is no *time* to consider.

Mayor You will deny it.

Stockmann Deny what?

Mayor Hovstad will have started the rumours already. You will go public tomorrow and deny them. You've conducted further tests and the situation is not as dangerous or as critical as you first thought.

Stockmann I'm speechless . . .

Mayor You have every confidence in the committee and every confidence that it will take the necessary steps to ensure the Baths are safe for public use.

Stockmann No. I won't do it.

Mayor You are forbidden as an employee to hold an opinion at variance with the committee.

Stockmann *Forbidden?*

Mayor You can hold private opinions but they must stay –

Stockmann I will not be gagged. I am a doctor.

Mayor I am your superior and you must obey.

Stockmann punches him. Petra runs in.

Petra Dad! Don't put up with this.

Mrs Stockmann (*following her in*) Petra!

Petra (*to Mayor*) Stop this!

Stockmann I will do nothing you ask.

Mayor Then your position will have to be reviewed.

Petra You'd sack him?

Mayor You would be forcing our hand.

Petra This is a disgrace! You're his brother . . .!

Mrs Stockmann Petra, be quiet.

Petra No, I will not!

Mayor Let her. She's always been encouraged to voice her feelings whenever she wants. You talk to him, Katrine, you're the only sensible one in this house. Make him –

Stockmann Leave my wife out of this.

Mayor Make him see this will affect you, the children –

Stockmann I said leave my –

Mayor The town –

Stockmann I am saving this town! I love this town!

Mayor But you'll happily destroy its only source of prosperity.

Stockmann The source is poisoned! Are you mad? Our prosperity comes from selling filth. Our whole communal life is based on a lie!

Mayor Pure make-believe. Or maybe something worse . . . Anyone who talks like that about his home town is an enemy of the town. A *public* enemy. You are a public enemy, Thomas.

Stockmann goes for him again.

Mrs Stockmann (*comes between them*) Thomas!

Petra Get out of our house! Get out!

Mayor I've warned you. You'll be ruined. Consider you wife. Consider you sons.

He leaves.

Mrs Stockmann Oh, this is horrible. Horrible.

Petra I could spit in his face.

Stockmann A public enemy? A public enemy? I'll make him regret that.

Mrs Stockmann He's the Mayor . . .

Petra So?

Stockmann I should do nothing? Is that your advice?

Mrs Stockmann You can't. He's the head of the town.

38

Stockmann I'm standing up for what is right.

Petra You have to, Dad. You must.

Stockmann Wait till you see what I'll do.

Mrs Stockmann You'll be sacked, Thomas. You heard him.

Petra Why do you always see everything from the family's point of view?

Mrs Stockmann You'll be all right – but the boys. And think of me as well.

Stockmann If I don't destroy those arrogant cowards . . .

Mrs Stockmann No money, Thomas, no food on the table. We were never going back to that, remember? I know this is terrible but it happens all the time . . . The boys, Thomas . . .

Eilif and Morten enter.

Stockmann I will not be intimidated! I will not be silenced!

Mrs Stockmann Please, Thomas . . .

Stockmann When they're grown men, I want to tell them what I did, not what I didn't do.

He walks out, slamming the door.

Mrs Stockmann (*crying*) God help us all.

Petra Dad is right. Dad is right. Dad is right.

Act Three

Editorial office of The Reformer. *Next door is the
printing room which can be seen through glass panels in
the wall. Hovstad is writing at his desk, which is littered
with documents, newspapers and books. A couple of
filthy, torn armchairs by a table; other old chairs
scattered about. Billing holds up Stockmann's report.*

Billing My God . . .

Hovstad Doesn't hold back, does he?

Billing It's an evisceration. Every sentence hits like a
hammer.

Hovstad It'll take more than a hammer . . .

Billing Who'd have thought? Dr Stockmann, leader of
the revolution.

Hovstad Shh . . . Aslaksen.

Billing Spineless . . . We are printing this, yes?

Hovstad Yes, if the Mayor decides to do nothing.

Billing Well, here's hoping he doesn't.

Hovstad It's good for us whatever happens. If he does
nothing, the small businessmen will hound him. If he
agrees to it, watch the Mayor's committee erupt.

Billing I want to see that.

Hovstad Either way, he's finished. But we must still drive
it home – incompetent, incapable. He must hand over
power immediately.

Billing Change finally! Revolution at last.

A knock on the door. Stockmann enters.

Hovstad Well?

Stockmann Print it.

Hovstad That's what I wanted to hear.

Billing Yes!

Stockmann It's war now, so print it.

Billing A fight to the death!

Stockmann (*indicates report*) This is only the start. I have four or five more articles I could write. Where's Aslaksen?

Billing (*shouts through*) Aslaksen!

Hovstad About the water system?

Stockmann No, there's other things I can expose – but they're all related. They all show the same contempt for the public. It will be like tearing down a building and discovering the foundations are rotten.

Billing I love the sound of that. Tearing down buildings.

Aslaksen (*enters*) What's being torn down? The Baths?

Hovstad No. Don't worry.

Billing Not yet . . .

Stockmann (*to Hovstad*) What did you make of my report?

Hovstad I think it's genius.

Stockmann It is, isn't it? Thank you.

Hovstad The argument is clear, lucid and easy to understand – even for a non-expert like myself. Anyone who reads it, anyone with an open mind, will be convinced by it.

Aslaksen Should we print it then ?

Hovstad The next edition.

Stockmann We can't afford to waste any more time. Mr Aslaksen, will you look after this? (*The report.*)

Aslaksen I'd be proud to.

Stockmann Guard it closely. (*To Hovstad.*) I'd like to proofread it before it goes to print. There can be no misprints or mistakes. I want every intelligent person to read this and be convinced.

Billing He puts us to shame . . .

Stockmann My own brother tried to shut me up. He threatened me – said they'd sack me.

Billing Sack you? Outrageous.

Stockmann It was like seeing him in a new light.

Hovstad Nothing he says would surprise me.

Stockmann He won't know what's hit him. I am going to attack and attack . . .

Aslaksen Now wait a moment . . .

Billing We're at war!

Stockmann Crush them all. Him and his –

Aslaksen Please, Dr Stockmann, show –

Billing Dynamite them! Wipe them out.

Stockmann It's not only the water and the sewer, it's the whole of society. It must be cleansed. Disinfected.

Billing Disinfected – the perfect word!

Stockmann All these men who have ruled us for so long – they must be wiped away. Root and branch. It's suddenly so clear to me, so . . . simple. We need young, strong, committed people to help us. To march alongside us, to fight with us. Do you agree?

Hovstad This is our chance to give power back to the people.

Aslaksen But sensibly – nothing too extreme . . .

Stockmann Who cares if it's extreme? We're doing this in the name of truth.

Hovstad You have our support, Doctor.

Aslaksen I suppose it is for the town. You do have its interests at heart.

Billing Dr Stockmann is fighting for the *people*.

Stockmann Thank you. Thank you. You don't know how good it is to hear that . . . I have to call on a patient now. Please take care of my manuscript. Goodbye for now.

Stockmann exits.

Hovstad He could be very useful to us.

Aslaksen As long as he keeps to the Baths. You can't let him go too far . . .

Billing You're always so bloody afraid . . .

Aslaksen When it involves the local authorities, yes, I am. I've seen what can happen. If this was the national government it would be different, I'd fight them all the way.

Billing You're a walking contradiction.

Aslaksen If you attack the government no harm's done. National politicians don't care. But overthrow the local authorities and you get idiots – anyone with half an opinion – suddenly taking control.

Hovstad We're fighting for the right of the people to govern *themselves*.

Aslaksen Let me tell you, when a man has interests of his own to protect that's *all* he thinks about.

Hovstad So we strip those men of their interests.

Billing Leave them with nothing.

Aslaksen I'd watch what you're saying, Mr Billing. Be very careful.

Billing What are you talking about?

Aslaksen I happen to know you've applied for an administrative position with the Council.

Hovstad *Have* you?

Billing Yes. But only to irritate them. Get up their noses.

Aslaksen It's not for me to judge. I've always endeavoured to be completely open about my views. I admit I am more of a moderate than I was, but that is the only charge anyone could level at me. My heart is still with the people but I also understand the difficult job the authorities have. The local ones, anyway. I do not believe that is cowardly or contradictory.

He walks through to the printing room.

Billing Can't we fire him?

Hovstad Who else do you know would give us credit on printing costs, paper . . .

Billing Stockmann?

Hovstad Stockmann has no money.

Billing But Morten Kiil's his father-in-law. And the money he rakes in . . .

Hovstad But we don't know if Stockmann sees any of it. We don't know anything . . .

Billing I was going to tell you.

Hovstad You know you won't get the job.

Billing Of course I won't. I don't have a chance. They'll have one of their own already lined up for it. I applied to remind myself how corrupt they *really* are, how nothing ever changes here.

Hovstad Yes, I'm sure you did.

Billing goes out. Petra enters, with the story she was to translate for Hovstad.

Petra.

Petra I hope I'm not interrupting?

Hovstad Not at all. Is it something from your father?

Petra I've come to give you this.

Hovstad You've translated it.

Petra No, I haven't. I don't want to.

Hovstad But . . .

Petra I agreed without reading it. You can't print this in the *Reformer*.

Hovstad Why not?

Petra You just can't. It's completely contrary to your opinions.

Hovstad Yes, but . . .

Petra A divine force which rewards the good and punishes the wicked. It's laughable. It's infantile.

Hovstad It's just a story – and people like to . . .

Petra You really want this in the *Reformer*?

Hovstad I can't always print what I want to.

Petra You're the editor.

Hovstad Who thinks about his readers. A bit of sentimental guff will send them back to the serious politics on the front pages.

Petra Oh, so you're hoodwinking them?

Hovstad (*smiles*) It was Billing's idea, not mine.

Petra Billing?

Hovstad Billing's full of surprises. Did you know he'd applied for a job within the Council?

Petra He wouldn't do that.

Hovstad Ask him yourself.

Petra Not Billing.

Hovstad Is it such a surprise?

Petra Yes. Or . . . Maybe not. I don't know . . .

Hovstad Hacks – we are not the noblest of creatures.

Petra You don't mean that.

Hovstad I do.

Petra You've taken up my father's cause.

Hovstad I have, yes.

Petra You're standing up for truth and courage. You're standing up for a wronged man.

Hovstad Yes, for a wronged man. And for you.

Petra For me? Am I all you care about?

Hovstad Is it such a surprise?

46

Petra Not being honest is what surprises me. Fighting for truth when all you want is . . .

Hovstad I can't have both?

Petra You disgust me.

Hovstad Do I? Are you sure?

Petra Yes, I'm sure.

Hovstad I'd watch what you're saying. Your father needs me. Look, I didn't mean that. I'm sorry.

She walks out. Aslaksen hurries in.

Aslaksen Hovstad . . .

Hovstad What?

Aslaksen The Mayor's come through the back, he wants to talk to you. He doesn't want to be seen.

The Mayor enters.

Mayor You must be surprised to see me here.

Hovstad Very.

Mayor I don't want to take up your time but something a little troubling happened today.

Hovstad What would that be?

Mayor My brother wrote a report concerning some defects in the Baths' water system.

Hovstad Really?

Mayor He hasn't told you about it? Funny, he said he had . . .

Hovstad I remember now, he did mention it briefly.

Aslaksen Excuse me, I need to . . . (*Takes Stockmann's report.*)

Mayor That's it. That's the report I'm talking about.

Hovstad Oh, *that's* it?

Mayor Yes, that's it. So you've read it?

Hovstad I glanced through it.

Mayor And are you publishing it?

Hovstad We're a liberal newspaper, we encourage all kinds of opinions.

Aslaksen Sir, I have absolutely no influence on the *Reformer*'s content.

Mayor No, I understand that.

Aslaksen I only print what I'm given.

Mayor I understand.

Aslaksen If you'll excuse me . . .

He moves towards the printing room.

Mayor One moment. You're the Chair of the Small Business Federation, aren't you?

Aslaksen I am, sir, yes.

Mayor You're well respected. I know about you.

Aslaksen I do my best for the small businessmen, sir.

Mayor Ah, small businesspeople. I must say I commend them.

Aslaksen I'll pass that on, sir.

Mayor I know money is tight but still . . . The sacrifice they're prepared to make . . .

Aslaksen I don't follow.

Hovstad What sacrifice?

Mayor It's a real mark of their commitment to this town. I can honestly say I wasn't expecting it. But you know them better than I do.

Aslaksen Sir, I . . .

Mayor Of course I shouldn't single them out, the whole town must share the burden.

Hovstad What burden?

Mayor Hundreds of thousands. The provisional cost of what the Doctor's proposing.

Aslaksen That can't be the amount?

Mayor Well, no, you're right, it could be double that. In which case a municipal loan will have to be taken out.

Hovstad You can't ask the town to pay . . .?

Aslaksen Taxes will rise.

Mayor Banks tend to insist on a return. Loans are granted to be repaid.

Hovstad What about the Baths' shareholders?

Mayor The shareholders will say they've invested enough. No, I'm afraid if this goes ahead the entire town will have to fund it, simple as that.

Aslaksen Hovstad . . .

Hovstad Yes, I know.

Mayor And worse than that, we'll be forced to close the Baths. For up to two years. That's how long the work will take. At least.

Aslaksen But, sir, that is our business gone . . . How are we supposed to survive?

Mayor It's very tricky. Very tricky. But what other option do we have? When word gets out that our water is (*quotes*) 'polluted . . . that we live on plague soil . . . that the town is poisoned' – do you think we'll get even one visitor between now and when the work finishes?

Aslaksen He's proved nothing so far. This is only speculation.

Mayor I must say, like you, I am unconvinced.

Aslaksen It's a disgrace – scandalous – that the town doctor . . . I beg your pardon, sir.

Mayor My brother has always had an impetuous streak. It *is* scandalous, you're quite right.

Aslaksen You can't still support him?

Hovstad I . . . well, I'll have to . . .

Mayor I've written a few points down about this. A fair and practical solution for everyone.

Aslaksen Do you have it with you?

Mayor (*produces it from his pocket*) I do.

Aslaksen catches sight of Stockmann approaching.

Aslaksen It's Stockmann.

Mayor (*leaves*) Get rid of him. We're not done here yet.

Stockmann enters.

Hovstad Stockmann . . . (*To Aslaksen.*) If you would, thank you. We're pushed for time.

Stockmann Forgive my impatience.

Hovstad We haven't set the print yet.

Aslaksen Come back later. It will take a while.

Stockmann All right, well . . . Oh, there was something else I wanted to say.

Hovstad Can't it wait . . . ?

Stockmann When people read what I've written, when they realise how much time I've devoted to this . . .

Aslaksen Doctor . . .

Stockmann I know what you're going to say. It's only a citizen doing as a citizen should – I agree. But the people of this town, you see, they admire me . . .

Aslaksen They have until now.

Stockmann But what if they take matters into their own hands?

Hovstad Doctor, I'm not going to lie . . .

Stockmann Aha, I knew there was something! I don't want it. You must put a stop to it.

Hovstad A stop to what?

Stockmann To them thanking me. Whether it's a gift or a dinner to thank me, you must stop them. I don't want that. You too, Aslaksen, tell them no.

Hovstad Doctor, I have to tell you something.

Mrs Stockmann enters.

Mrs Stockmann I was right. I knew it.

Stockmann What are you doing here?

Mrs Stockmann You really can't think why? You have three children back at home . . .

Stockmann Katrine, I'm on important business.

Mrs Stockmann Thomas, you need to –

Aslaksen Be sensible. I've told him that.

Mrs Stockmann I don't appreciate my husband being used as a pawn in your eternal campaign against authority, Mr Hovstad.

Stockmann A pawn? I'm not stupid.

Mrs Stockmann You're clever, Thomas but you're also naive. (*To Hovstad.*) You know they'll dismiss him if you print his report?

Stockmann (*laughs*) They can try – but I have the majority on my side.

Mrs Stockmann You think that will help you?

Stockmann Go back home, Katrine. Let us do what we have to do. We're fighting for the truth here.

He sees the Mayor's hat.

This is Peter's. Is he here? Peter?

Aslaksen He's left. He's gone.

Stockmann No, he hasn't. Are you *hiding*? (*Roars with laughter.*) Come out, you coward! Come out.

The Mayor enters. Billing follows him.

Mayor No need to shout, Thomas.

Stockmann I want to shout! I want to shout at you. We're starting a revolution, Peter, so get used to it. Hovstad will shout, Billing will shout. Aslaksen and all his small businesses will shout.

Aslaksen No, I won't, sir. I won't be part of it.

Stockmann Of course you will . . .

Mayor Hovstad, have you decided?

Hovstad I'm sorry, Dr Stockmann.

Aslaksen Mr Hovstad is not so stupid that he'd destroy himself and the *Reformer* for the sake of your delusions.

Stockmann What do you mean, 'delusions'?

Hovstad You've stated your case falsely, Doctor. We can't support you.

Stockmann Well then, print my article and I will defend it on my own.

Hovstad No, I won't.

Stockmann You're the editor! You have control.

Aslaksen Our readers have control. Public opinion controls newspapers.

Mayor Which is as it should be.

Aslaksen It would destroy the town if your article was printed.

Stockmann So you definitely won't print it? That's your last word?

Hovstad We're protecting you and your family . . .

Mrs Stockmann We do not *need* protecting, Mr Hovstad.

Mayor (*to Aslaksen*) Print what I've given you.

Aslaksen nods, starts to go next door.

Stockmann Aslaksen, I want my report printed as a pamphlet. I want four hundred, no, five . . . no, I want six hundred printed. I will pay whatever it costs.

Aslaksen No, sir, I can't let my press be used for that.

Stockmann Then give me it back.

Hovstad hands it back.

I will make this heard, don't doubt that. I'll hire a hall, distribute the information and read it aloud myself.

Mayor You will have some difficulty doing that, Thomas.

Aslaksen You won't find anyone who'll support you.

Mrs Stockmann (*takes Stockmann's arm*) I will. I will support you. I'm on your side, Thomas.

Stockmann Thank you, Katrine. If I can't find anywhere, I will go through the streets myself and read it aloud on street corners.

Mayor For God's sake, this is madness.

Stockmann Then I am mad.

Billing There, he's said it. He's admitted it.

Aslaksen No one will listen to you.

Mrs Stockmann The boys will listen to you. And Petra. And me. We will all listen.

Stockmann (*kisses her*) Now we have a fight, gentlemen.

They leave.

Mayor He's driven her mad as well.

Act Four

The hall in Captain Horster's house.
Stockmann with Mrs Stockmann, Petra and the boys.
Also, the Mayor, Hovstad, Billing, Aslaksen and Horster.
Stockmann stands up to address a large assembled
audience of people from all social classes. He opens his
mouth to speak but is immediately interrupted by Aslaksen.

Billing We have no chairman. We must have a chairman.

Stockmann There's no need for a chairman.

Billing A chairman has to be elected before you can
begin.

Stockmann This is a lecture. I'm delivering a lecture.

Billing Due process demands that we elect a chairman.

Stockmann Very well. Let due process have its way.

Aslaksen Is the Mayor willing to serve as chairman?

Mayor Thank you, but no. It would not be appropriate
for me to serve as chairman. You all have to listen to me
so much you must be sick of my voice. Looking around
the room, I see several . . . Mr Aslaksen. I nominate you
as chairman.

Aslaksen Thank you. I accept. Everyone here knows
me, quiet, unassuming – a man who values good sense
and sobriety above all else. I would therefore ask Dr
Stockmann that he respect good sense and sobriety and
behaves accordingly. Before Dr Stockmann speaks, has
anyone anything to say? . . . The Mayor.

Mayor I'm in a somewhat delicate position. As you all know, my brother is the Chief Medical Officer of the Baths. I would really rather not have to speak now but my position as Head of the Council – and with the town's interests at heart – I am reluctantly forced to table a resolution. It's obvious that no one present wants the Doctor's unreliable and exaggerated report to spread beyond this room tonight – the damage it would inflict is incalculable. In my article in today's *Reformer* I outlined the essential facts of the case. For those of you who haven't read it, the Doctor's proposal – apart from containing what amounts to a vote of no confidence in the leading men of this town – will burden the taxpayer with the outlandish expense of at least – at *least* – one hundred thousand crowns. The assertion that our Baths are poisoned is utter, utter nonsense. My resolution is straight-forward. I move that this meeting prohibit the Medical Officer from reading aloud or promoting his report.

Aslaksen We all recognise the Doctor is diligent, hard-working and much liked but he can be rash, wrong-headed and, though it pains me to remind you of it, attracted to subversion. He wants to wrest control from the very same authorites that we elect. I am all for increased self-government, but not if it inflicts crippling financial consequences on small businesses. This is what would happen if the Doctor is indulged tonight. This is why I second the Mayor's resolution.

Hovstad I am one of Dr Stockmann's supporters and friends, but I am sorry to say I have been misled by a distorted report . . .

Stockmann *Distorted?* How is my report distorted?

Hovstad It is clearly biased. The Mayor's piece that we printed today shows that. You must realise now, Doctor, public opinion is completely against you. As editor of the *Reformer* I must reflect the views of my readers and

I must keep their best interests at heart. It has caused me great pain breaking with the Doctor over this – I've been a guest in his home; I've eaten at his table. I'm not alone in my respect and admiration for him, even if he does follow his heart more than his head. But he must understand my duty to this community comes first. I am also concerned, Doctor, about this line you're taking . . . Think of your family . . .

Mrs Stockmann Leave my family out of this!

Aslaksen I must now put the Mayor's resolution to the vote. Raise your hands all those in favour of prohibiting the Doctor . . .

Stockmann raises his hand.

Stockmann I'm in favour, Mr Chairman! I support the Mayor's resolution. Here is my report.

He holds it up. And then tears it into pieces.

Forget the Baths. Forget the poisoned water. Forget plague-ridden soil. Because I have made a greater discovery. It is our *spiritual* lives which are poisoned. Our whole community is built on a plague-ridden soil of lies and hypocrisy.

Billing You were asked to moderate your language.

Stockmann The great pity is – I love this town. When I lived in the north, I felt incredible nostalgia for it – and for you, you the people I grew up with. The north is nasty, brutal, punitive. The people there: desperate, abject, pitiful. What they needed actually was not a doctor but a vet.

Billing That's disgraceful.

Hovstad That's an insult to decent people.

Stockmann There wasn't a *day* when I didn't think of returning here. I ached, I yearned to come home. I had great plans. I had great ideas for this town. How deluded was I? How misguided to entrust my vision of the Baths to my brother and his Council? What do we – we, all of us here – what do we think about politicians? What's our view of men who distort, equivocate, hoodwink, misrepresent and lie? Men who can't open their mouths without lying? Men who lie to us, lie to each other and who lie even to themselves? Who lie because they know that the political system, without which they have no power, cannot function if they tell the truth? Has anyone here one good word to say about politicians? Anyone? Show of hands? I of course speak from personal experience of one of our better known examples. My brother, Peter. Take a bow, Peter. No applause? Come on . . . (*He begins to applaud.*) Applaud your dutiful public servant. Thank you, Peter. But why bother denouncing politicians – ludicrous representatives of values that ought to be dead and buried. All of them digging their own graves. All of them on a suicide mission to obscurity. They don't need a doctor like me to put them out of their misery. It's not politicians who we ought to fear. No, there is an even greater danger which pollutes and poisons our community. Anyone guess what it is? It's *you*. You, the majority. You are the enemies of truth. The majority. You.

Aslaksen Withdraw those remarks.

Hovstad The majority is always right.

Stockmann 'The majority is always right' . . . Who makes up the majority of inhabitants in a country? Ask yourselves that? Is it clever people or stupid people? Anyone here disagree that the number of stupid people in the world far outnumbers the clever? You all agree with that, don't you? In your hearts. In your hearts. So should the stupid be allowed to rule over the clever for all time? Who here believes the majority is always right? Let's have a show of hands. That belief is a lie that every free man must fight. The majority has power, yes, but that doesn't make the majority right. The minority – the men who see things from a different angle, the men who are true to what they see, who dare to disagree with how the stupid majority see the world – *we* are right. In fact – and this is entirely logical – the minority is always right.

Hovstad So Dr Stockmann has become an elitist?

Stockmann (*points at the Mayor*) No, he's the elitist! All he cares about is that power stays in *his* hands. That's all he cares about. But as I said, I won't waste breath talking about him. The future won't include him. The minority *I* am referring to are the few, brave individuals with the courage to stand apart from the herd, who feel which way the wind is blowing. For whom received wisdom is like rotten food. Visionaries who are unafraid of revolutionary ideas, of new truths. Men who are years and years ahead of the rest – battling for truths which are not yet born, which are just coming into being, ideas which, it's no stretch of the imagination to say, will *never* occur to you, not in your lifetime. And you – you, ladies and gentlemen – if you are ignorant and left behind, you have only yourselves to blame. What you will have failed to understand is that truth is a living thing, it responds, it evolves. Or . . . it grows stale. It can fossilise. It can rot and stink. Yet despite the putrid stench of *your* truth, of what *you* think of as truth, you grimly cradle it like comfort blankets, like cuddly toys. You relish the slops that Granny dished up for us when we were young which you've never lost the taste for. Any grannies in tonight? Granny is long dead. Granny's been eaten by worms six feet under. But you, the majority, won't let her rest in peace.

The Mayor starts to go.

Mayor This is embarassing. I'm so sorry. The speaker's gone off the rails. He's off his head.

Hovstad The majority value democracy, thank God. The same democracy that regrettably allows the speaker to voice his offensive beliefs.

Stockmann Thank you, Mr Hovstad, for voicing *your* offensive beliefs. Let's be clear about this. Democracy has nothing to do with responsible choices but with *popular* choices. Democracy puts power in the hands of large numbers of ignorant, unimaginative individuals who have not the slightest understanding of which ideas are healthy for the community. How could they have? Does an ant know there is life outside the ant heap?

Hovstad Oh, so we're ants now?

Stockmann What is democracy? I'll tell you what democracy is. It is the majority voting for ideas that are selfish and egotistical, ideas that promote personal gain over the wellbeing of the planet, ideas which are incapable of creating a long-term future for all of us. Just because something is popular, does that mean it's good? A new product on the market turns out to be garbage, a pressure group just downright crazy, a leader psychotic – but everyone loves them so questions are never asked. The way we live, popularity justifies any behaviour, any at all, and that's why no morality can withstand the – excuse me – gang rape of democracy. After all, what is gang rape? The majority getting what it wants. The truth has to struggle night and day. The howling of the masses will always drown out the trumpet of reason. I expected more of you, Mr Hovstad. You never stop letting us know how progressive you are. Truth must never be the servant of money. That's one of your wise sayings, I seem to remember.

Hovstad When did I ever say that – in print?

Stockmann True. You never had the guts. I don't like to embarrass you with your failings, Mr Hovstad, but someone has to. It makes me vomit the way you bow down before the masses as if they were sacred. Day after day your newspaper – which claims to be progressive – claims also to embody the people's will. This is a lie! Hovstad doesn't realise it, but what he wants is exactly the same as the politicians want, as my brother wants. He doesn't want you to think for yourselves, to have your own ideas. He doesn't want you to be individuals, to aspire to deeper, more complex, more meaningful lives. How are we doing? Are you receiving me loud and clear? The politicians and the peddlers of newspapers are very happy for you to remain exactly as you are. Are you happy to remain as you are? They have convinced you – him and him and others like them – that all is well, all is good. Now they want to convince you that everything you do and say and feel and believe has *value*, as much value as the thoughts and beliefs and feelings of a highly trained doctor and scientist. He wants to convince you that ignorance and stupidity are just as precious as curiosity and achievement. Are you going to believe him? Are you one of those people who are flattered, delighted, relieved when you hear this? Who say 'I haven't worked hard, I haven't studied, I have no ambition – but who cares? I'm as good as anyone else.' The world is full of wonderful things – art, culture, science. But they need effort to understand, so lazy people prefer the cheap and the vulgar and the simple-minded. Men of genius have achieved some understanding of nature, of how things are, the secrets of life. But you let him and him persuade you that the only thing that matters is how big is the waistline of your favourite film star, or has a shipping magnate got a secret wife? The international tittle-tattle of the gossip columns which masquerades as meaningful life. You're addicted to these politicians who tell you that the clothes you wear, the cars you drive, the houses you live in, mean something about yourselves rather than about the people who made them, and how they were made, and who profited. If this is what you get by voting for them, don't vote! Keep your dignity. Don't take part in this fraudulent system. Join the non-voting party. I never vote. Where does it lead? To the graveyard of civilisation. You want to live decent, generous lives, lives of value to the people you love and respect. The obvious truth is that if that's truly what you want, then what you need to do is to control, to contain, to repress – either by law or custom – the inherent tendency in human nature towards brutality, towards barbarism. I've never heard one of your politicians say anything like that. Over the last two days I have seen civilised standards deliberately trashed by cynical politicians – and by men like Hovstad. Were you to be looking for the lair of evil – the evil of human beings doing whatever the hell they please with no fear of law and without a shred of conscience – you've come to the right place. These men are dragging you into the void! And who is protesting? They want to steal your humanity, your individuality! Not one of you understands what is happening!

Billing Get him off! Grab him. Shout him down. Off! Off!

Kiil I need to ask something. Where are you telling us that the poison comes from?

Stockmann From the swamp in Molledalen.

Kiil From my tannery too?

Stockmann I will hide nothing. From your tannery too. I will shout this from every street corner! I will write articles and publish them in every newspaper across the country! I will tell the whole country that the water is poisoned! I will tell the whole country that the Baths are full of plague! I love this town, but I will destroy it rather than let it live on lies! A community that lives on lies deserves to be destroyed! It should be razed to the ground. You should be exterminated like vermin, all of you, before you poison the whole country. And if it happens that the whole country *is* poisoned, the whole country must be flattened, the whole population wiped out – and it is you who will be responsible!

Aslaksen I want to propose a resolution. That all present consider Dr Stockmann to be a public enemy. Raise your hands all those who . . .

Stockmann No, I will propose that resolution. I am an enemy of the majority. You don't need to raise your hands. I'm raising mine. I am a public enemy! I am your enemy. I am a public enemy! I am a public enemy!

Act Five

*Stockmann's study. Bookshelves. Cupboards with
medicines inside. The windows are smashed. Stockmann
in dressing gown and slippers is bent over raking a small
rock out from under a cupboard. He adds it to a pile of
them on his writing desk.*

Stockmann Another one.

Mrs Stockmann What are you doing?

Stockmann Building a sacred monument to ignorance.
I want the boys to see it every day. Has the girl gone for
the window repairman yet?

Mrs Stockmann I've already told you. He's refusing to
come.

Stockmann He's too scared to. Coward.

Mrs Stockmann (*hands him a letter*) This came.

Stockmann (*reads it*) Our landlord giving us notice.

Mrs Stockmann Oh . . .

Stockmann 'It is with regret . . . I have no option . . . My
apologies.' We don't give a damn, do we? We're leaving
for the other side of the world.

Mrs Stockmann Thomas, the United States of America
are so far away . . .

Stockmann How can I stay? I'm a public enemy. I'm
hated. People are smashing our windows with rocks!
Look, my trousers are ripped.

Mrs Stockmann They were so expensive.

Stockmann When you fight for freedom, never wear expensive trousers. I can still see their idiotic faces bawling at me like they were my equals.

Mrs Stockmann Yes, they've treated you badly – but the United States of America, Thomas . . .

Stockmann It will be no different anywhere else in this country – the people here are mindless slaves. It may well be the same in the United States – the same majority and liberal public opinion and who knows what else? But it's on a much bigger scale across there. They might kill you but they won't torture you. They won't take a free man and destroy his soul. And if doesn't work out there, we'll move on to the next place. If I could I'd buy a jungle somewhere or a South Sea island . . .

Mrs Stockmann I'm only thinking about the boys.

Stockmann You want them to grow up here? You want them to become men who walk around in herds telling themselves they are free-thinkers?

Mrs Stockmann I know, Thomas, but . . .

Petra enters.

What are you doing back so early?

Petra I've been sacked.

Mrs Stockmann Sacked?

Petra The head teacher gave me a week's notice, but I decided to leave immediately.

Stockmann You did exactly the right thing.

Mrs Stockmann But the head teacher thought so much of you . . .

Petra She had no choice. The school has already received three letters of complaint about me.

Stockmann (*laughs, rubs his hands*) 'She had no choice' . . . The town has descended into madness. The letters were anonymous, I take it?

Petra Of course.

Stockmann Not even the guts to sign their names.

Petra They complained I have unconventional views on a number of significant issues.

Stockmann You didn't deny it?

Petra Of course not, Dad.

Stockmann Start packing now. I refuse to live amongst this ludicrous hypocrisy. The sooner we leave the better.

Mrs Stockmann Quiet. There's someone in the hall. Go and look, Petra.

Petra (*at the door*) Captain Horster . . . Please, come in.

Horster Good afternoon. I thought I'd look in. How are you all?

Stockmann Thank you, Johan. Good of you to come.

Mrs Stockmann I never thanked you for your help.

Petra You got home safely after the meeting?

Horster Safe enough. I can look after myself. They were all mouth, no action.

Stockmann The cowards. Look at these. Stones they threw through our windows. There's a few decent-sized ones – this one's the biggest. But the rest are pebbles. And look . . . They stood outside, screaming with fury that they were going to beat me up – and all they throw is *gravel*?

Horster I'd be thankful for that.

Stockmann But what if one day they *really* had to fight for something . . . That's what saddens me; that is what's so deeply painful. I can't be sentimental. If they want me to be a public enemy, then I may as well be one.

Mrs Stockmann Don't say that, Thomas. I don't like it.

Stockmann I can't get the words out my head – they're lodged in here, just beneath my heart and they're painful.

Petra Laugh at them, Dad. Just laugh at them.

Horster I'm sure they'll change their minds soon enough.

Mrs Stockmann Of course they will. Johan's right, Thomas. They can't keep this up.

Stockmann Too late. It will be too late. They'll have driven me out and they'll be sorry. When do we sail?

Horster That is the reason I've come.

Stockmann Is there something wrong with the ship?

Petra They've sacked you as well, haven't they?

Horster Yes, indeed they have.

Petra You and me.

Mrs Stockmann Do you hear that, Thomas?

Stockmann If I thought this would happen . . .

Horster Don't worry about that. I'll find work with another shipping line.

Petra This wouldn't have happened if you hadn't helped us.

Horster I don't regret it for a moment.

Petra Thank you.

Horster I have an idea I wanted to put to you . . .

Stockmann Good, good. I want us to leave as soon as we can.

Mrs Stockmann Was that the door?

Petra (*opens it*) It's Uncle . . . It's the Mayor.

Stockmann Aha. (*Shouts.*) Come in.

Mrs Stockmann Thomas, don't make it any worse.

The Mayor enters.

Mayor Ah. Are you busy?

Stockmann No, no. Come on. Come in.

Mayor I'd like to speak with you alone.

Mrs Stockmann We will go next door. Petra.

Horster I can come back later.

Stockmann No, go with them. I'll talk to you after he's gone.

Horster leaves with Mrs Stockmann and Petra. The Mayor looks out the window, saying nothing.

Stockmann There's a slight draught. I'd put your hat on.

Mayor Thank you. I think I caught a cold last night. It was freezing in that hall. (*Indicates the window.*) I regret it is not in my power to prevent this.

Stockmann Was there anything specific you wanted to say to me?

Mayor (*produces a letter*) From the Baths Committee.

Stockmann Ah, my dismissal, I assume.

Mayor Effective immediately. We're sorry but we had no choice . . .

Stockmann No choice . . .

Mayor Also, it will be difficult for you to continue practising here. The small businessmen have started a campaign to boycott you and people are queueing up to sign it.

Stockmann I wouldn't expect otherwise.

Mayor If I can give you some advice? I would leave here for a while.

Stockmann I'm ahead of you there. Plans have already been made.

Mayor Good. I'd take six months or so, reflect on what's happened and then perhaps you could . . .

Stockmann I could . . . ?

Mayor If you were to write a few words of regret admitting the mistake you've made.

Stockmann And I'd . . . what? Be reinstated?

Mayor It's certainly not impossible.

Stockmann But there's public opinion . . . What about public opinion? What would it have to say about my reinstatement?

Mayor Public opinion is a very fickle thing. And to be honest with you, it is very important that we have a written admission from you.

Stockmann I'm sure it is . . . You've tried this before, don't you remember? The retraction you wanted me to write?

Mayor Things were different then – that was when you thought you had the whole town behind you.

Stockmann Now I have the whole town on top of me, crushing me. I won't do it. I will never do it.

Mayor You are a man with a family to provide for – you have a responsibility.

Stockmann Do you know what my responsibility is? My responsibility is to teach my family that the truth should be honoured above all else.

Mayor Very noble. There's another reason, isn't there? There's another reason you're doing this.

Stockmann What do you mean?

Mayor You know what I'm talking about. I'd be careful if I were you. Things can easily go wrong.

Stockmann I don't know what you're talking about.

Mayor Morten. The will he's had drawn up. You don't know about it? You're telling me you know nothing about it?

Stockmann I know what money he has will go to a foundation for his workers when they retire. What's that to do with me?

Mayor What money he has . . . ? We're not talking small amounts. Morten is a seriously wealthy man.

Stockmann I've never really dwelt on it.

Mayor Really? Come on, Thomas . . . He hasn't told you a large part of his money will go to your children?

Stockmann No.

Mayor You and Katrine will be able to live very comfortably from the interest.

Stockmann I swear to you he's never mentioned it. All he talks about is how high you tax him. Are you sure about this?

Mayor There's very little I don't know about this town.

Stockmann Thank God. Katrine will have some security then. And the children. I have to tell her.

Mayor Wait. Don't say anything yet.

Stockmann They're safe . . . They're safe.

Mayor That's exactly what you aren't. Katrine is his stepdaughter. Morten can annul the will any time he wants.

Stockmann But he won't. He agrees with me about the Baths. He *wanted* me to take you all on.

Mayor Ah. Well, that explains a few things.

Stockmann What things?

Mayor The two of you are together in this. The smears, the violent attacks you've made on myself and the committee.

Stockmann What about them?

Mayor To keep you in his will . . . That vindictive old man played the tune and you danced.

Stockmann (*speechless for a moment*) Peter. You are scum. You are the lowest of the low.

Mayor Everything is over between us – *everything*. I'll make sure you are never reinstated. You will never practise again. We have this over you now.

    He exits.

Stockmann Scum. Scum. Katrine, wash the floor! Tell the girl to bring a bucket and scrub this floor!

Mrs Stockmann (*enters, with Petra*) Thomas, shh . . .

Petra Dad.

Stockmann What?

Petra Grandfather's here. He wants to talk to you.

Morten Kiil enters. Petra and Mrs Stockmann go.

Kiil Fresh air is good for you. How are you today?

Stockmann I'm fine.

Kiil Good. You'll need to be. I have something here.

He holds up a bundle of shares.

Stockmann Shares in the Baths?

Kiil Yes. Going for a song.

Stockmann You *bought* them?

Kiil I bought as many as I could afford.

Stockmann Morten, in a few days they'll be worthless . . .

Kiil And if you're smart, they may not be worthless.

Stockmann I've done all I can to save the Baths – no one will listen . . . The people of this town are mad.

Kiil You said yesterday that the worst muck, the worst shit comes from my tannery. That means, if it was true, that my grandfather and my father and now me have been poisoning this town for three generations. Did you not think before you opened your mouth? You really expect me to take it lying down?

Stockmann I'm afraid you have to accept it.

Kiil No, I don't accept it. I want to keep my good name, my reputation. I'm well aware people call me the Skunk – I want to know who named me that . . . No one has *any* right to call me that. I want to live and to die with my name clean.

Stockmann And how will you do that?

Kiil You will do it. You will make me clean.

Stockmann Me?

Kiil (*holds up the shares*) Do you know what I bought these with? You won't. With the money that Katrine, Petra and the boys were to get from me. I had put some aside for them, you see.

Stockmann You've spent their money on shares in the Baths?

Kiil Yes. All their money is now invested in the Baths. I want to see if you really are mad, Thomas. If you keep mouthing off about my tannery and the poisoned water, then you will be inflicting a life of poverty on your wife and your children. Now, who'd do a thing like that – the head of a family – unless he was a madman?

Stockmann Yes, but I am a madman. I am a madman.

Kiil You are not that insane – your wife, your children . . .

Stockmann Why didn't you speak to me before you did this?

Kiil I've only done what needed doing.

Stockmann But I'm so sure. I am so sure I'm right.

Kiil If you keep saying that, these will be worth nothing.

Stockmann But, damn it, there must be something, some chemical that could purify the water.

Kiil Something to kill off all those nasty animals that no one can see.

Stockmann Yes, or render them harmless.

Kiil What about rat poison?

Stockmann They all think I imagined this. That I made it up. All right, let them. Let them be right. I did. I imagined it.

Kiil I'd wait a day or two before replacing your windows, to be on the safe side.

Stockmann I have to talk to Katrine. She'll know what to do.

Kiil Do that. Listen to her. Listen to the advice of a sensible woman.

Stockmann (*rushes towards him*) That is their money! They're your grandchildren! You devil!

Kiil I want your answer by two. Yes or no. If it is no, the shares will go the foundation.

Stockmann And Katrine will get nothing?

Kiil Nothing. Not a penny.

The hall door opens. Hovstad and Aslaksen are there.

Look who we have here. Two o'clock. Yes or no.

Kiil leaves.

Stockmann What do you want? Make it brief.

Hovstad I understand you'll be angry with us for our attitude yesterday . . .

Stockmann Attitude? You call that attitude? I call it spineless and pathetic.

Hovstad You can call it what you want. We could do nothing else.

Stockmann You couldn't, could you? Is that right? You could do nothing?

Hovstad No, we couldn't.

Aslaksen But why didn't you drop a hint beforehand? Just a small hint to Mr Hovstad or me.

Stockmann A hint? What about?

Aslaksen What was behind it all.

Stockmann Behind what? I don't understand.

Aslaksen Yes, you do, Doctor, you understand fully.

Hovstad No need to keep it secret now.

Stockmann What the hell is this?

Aslaksen Can I ask . . .? It is true Morten Kiil's been buying up shares in the Baths?

Stockmann Yes, he has been buying shares, yes, but . . .

Aslaksen You should have been smarter. You should have used someone else – someone not so close to you.

Hovstad You should have taken your name off the report. No one needed to know you'd written it. You should have talked to me before you did anything.

Stockmann Taken my name off the report? Could I have done that? Is it possible to do that?

Aslaksen As long as it's done discreetly.

Hovstad You should've involved more people, Doctor. Cast your net a bit wider. Reduces the risk.

Stockmann Get to the point. Tell me what you want.

Aslaksen Hovstad's probably better placed to . . .

Hovstad No, you tell him.

Aslaksen Well, the thing is, now that we understand how everything . . . fits, we want you to know that the *Reformer*'s door is open to you.

Stockmann Open?

Hovstad Open wide.

Stockmann But . . . Are you sure? Will the storm of protest not be deafening?

Hovstad We can ride any storm.

Aslaksen But you should be quick. Whilst your attack is still exercising people . . .

Stockmann Morten and I should buy up the remaining shares – that's what you mean?

Hovstad Of course it's purely for scientific reasons that you want the Baths, isn't it? Am I right?

Stockmann Naturally. Scientific reasons, yes. That's how I got the Skunk to agree to come in with me. We'll tinker around with the pipes, dig up the beach a bit, make it look official. It won't cost the taxpayers a penny. We should be able to pull it off, don't you think?

Hovstad With the *Reformer* behind you, you definitely could.

Aslaksen In a free society, Doctor, the press is power.

Stockmann What about the small businesses, won't they . . . ?

Aslaksen Leave them to me. I'll handle them.

Stockmann Gentlemen, I'm . . . It's awkward, but what about payment? Some kind of fee for you both?

Hovstad No, we don't want any payment. But as you know, the *Reformer* isn't in the best state of health. I would hate to see it close down now when we have so much more to fight for politically.

Stockmann Of course. It must be hard for a man like yourself. A champion of the people. But I am the public enemy . . . And if I paid you nothing? Not a penny. Us wealthy people like to keep hold of their riches, you know.

Hovstad This whole shares thing will have to be handled very carefully. One wrong step, one slip . . .

Stockmann And you are just the man who'd do that, Mr Hovstad. If I don't help the *Reformer*, your position will magically change and you will hunt me down, won't you? You'll come after me – like dogs after a rabbit. Tear me apart.

Aslaksen It's natural law, Dr Stockmann. More dog eat dog, I'd say.

Hovstad Survival at any cost.

Stockmann picks up an umbrella and attacks them with it.

Stockmann Get out! Get out!

Mrs Stockmann, Petra and Horster enter.

Mrs Stockmann Thomas . . . !

Stockmann Jump! Out of the window. Into the gutter.

Mrs Stockmann Control yourself.

The two men exit.

What is going on?

Stockmann is already writing on a piece of paper. He holds it up.

Stockmann Read out what this says.

Mrs Stockmann 'No, no, no.'

Stockmann Petra, get the girl to deliver this to Morten now.

Petra Yes, Dad.

Petra exits with the piece of paper.

Stockmann Well, the devil's sent his messengers today, hasn't he? I'm going to sharpen my pen, as sharp as a knife and I'm going to dip it in ink and cut them in two. Cut them to pieces.

Mrs Stockmann But, Thomas, I thought we were leaving?

Petra (*returns*) It's done.

Stockmann Leaving? No, we're staying. We're staying to fight. We have to find a house for the winter.

Horster You're welcome to my father's old place. Plenty of room there. I won't bother you.

Mrs Stockmann That is very kind of you, Captain Horster.

Stockmann Yes, thank you. And now I have to . . . Katrine, I've been sacked as Medical Officer.

Mrs Stockmann It's hardly a surprise.

Stockmann And I have no practice any more. They can do what they want. The destitute can still come to me, those who can pay nothing. They are the ones who need me the most. I will preach to them what I believe – and they will listen to me, damn it!

Mrs Stockmann Thomas, you've seen where preaching gets you . . .

Stockmann I don't understand you, Katrine. I should let myself be beaten by them? What I have to say is so obvious and simple and straightforward. Those political men, they kill truth. They strangle every new idea. And morality. And justice. They'll bring terror to this town. Surely I can make them understand that, Johan?

Horster Perhaps. Who knows?

Stockmann The party leaders must be hunted down and exterminated. They're wolves – ravenous wolves who need to devour more and more victims to survive. And Hovstad and Aslaksen? How many have they devoured? Or torn them to pieces so they're no use for anything except to become small businessmen or subscribe to the *Reformer*? Come here, Katrine, come here. Look at the sunlight coming through the window. And do you feel that wonderful spring air?

Mrs Stockmann If only we could live on it. Eat it and drink it.

Stockmann We'll have to watch our money, but that's fine, we've done it before. My main worry is who will continue my work after me?

Petra The boys, Father. You'll be able to teach the boys.

Stockmann I will.

Eilif and Morten enter.

Mrs Stockmann Why are you home so early?

Morten We were in a fight.

Eilif That's not true – you started a fight. We were sent home.

Stockmann You're never going back there. You won't set foot in that school again.

Mrs Stockmann But Thomas . . .

Stockmann I'll teach you myself. You may not learn much but what you will learn is how to be free, independent men. You will help me, Petra.

Petra Of course I will, Dad.

Stockmann Classes will take place in Captain Horster's house, let's see how they like that . . . But we need more pupils. We need at least a dozen pupils to start with.

Mrs Stockmann You won't find any here.

Stockmann We'll see. They have to be destitute, impoverished children.

Petra I know some. I'll find them for you.

Stockmann Good. Get them; bring them here. I'm going to teach them. I'm going to see what these mongrels are capable of. (*To the boys.*) You are the first pupils of the Academy for Free Men.

Morten We're going to be free men!

Stockmann You're going to hunt down all the wolves, boys, drive them out to the far west.

Mrs Stockmann I hope it won't be the wolves hunting you.

Stockmann Me? Are you mad? I am the strongest man in this town.

Mrs Stockmann The strongest?

Stockmann Yes, the strongest. I'm one of the strongest men in the world.

Morten Really?

Stockmann (*lowers his voice*) Shh. Don't tell anyone yet but I've made a discovery today.

Mrs Stockmann Thomas, don't . . .

Stockmann But I have. I have. The strongest man in the world is the man who stands alone. I am that man. I stand alone. I am the strongest man. I am the strongest man in the world.